VIEWS
FROM THE
EDUCATION
UNDERGROUND

AS ZACH CLEMENTS SEES IT

VIEWS FROM THE EDUCATION UNDERGROUND

AS ZACH CLEMENTS SEES IT

Rich Publishing Co.

10611 Creektree • Houston, Texas 77070

First Edition 1990
First Printing, January 1990
Second Printing, September 1992

Library of Congress Catalog Card No. 89-61669
ISBN 0-9607256-8-7
Printed in the United States of America

ACKNOWLEDGEMENTS

I like to think I am a fair speaker, but as a writer I could never complete a presentable publication without a great deal of help from a large number of people. My wife, Cindy, has the patience of a saint and the editorial skills of her late newspaperman father. Sid Rauch, Professor of Reading Education at Hofstra University, has always provided honest criticism and the motivation to reach ever higher. Dorothy Rauch has often provided bed and board, along with tender support on those editorial retreats in Brooklyn. Peter Willis, a great writer and friend, never stints on his time, support and invaluable expertise in spotting weak writing and making insightful suggestions. A great many cartoons were reviewed by groups of educators throughout the land. For their efforts and those of their committees, I wish to extend my appreciation to the following:

Doug Pecina, Tom's River Schools, New Jersey; Jim Gibney, Falls River Schools, Massachusetts; Kathryn

Kelehear, Dalton Schools, Georgia; Joe Dripps, Clinton Community Schools, DeWitt, Iowa; Terry Brooks, Jefferson County Schools, Louisville, Kentucky; Al Slawson, Tucson Schools, Arizona; John Still, Pinellas County Schools, Clearwater, Florida; Jim Hill, Little Falls Schools, Minnesota; Julie Adams, Fresno Schools, California; Don Whalen, Long Beach City Schools, Lido Beach, New York; and, to Chris Copp for her initial efforts on the cartoon drawings.

To all these people and others I may have inadvertently omitted, my sincere thanks for making me look so good,

AND

For all of the above, the title, and so much more, I dedicate this book to you, Sid. I am so fortunate to be able to call you my friend and mentor.

Zach Clements

INTRODUCTION

S everal years ago my **serious** views of education were published. While I believe the book had merit, in no way did it advance the philosophy of laughter which is essential to an educator's well-being. Not so with *VIEWS FROM THE EDUCATION UNDERGROUND*. Here I offer iconoclastic views of my professional world in the hope they may elicit a chuckle or two.

More than three decades have gone by, yet it seems only yesterday a crew-cut young man in rumpled corduroy suit began his love affair with schools in an urban junior high. There is no VIEW of life quite like that afforded the classroom teacher of students in their early teens — kids being propelled into puberty and hurled onward towards maturity at mean rates of acceleration ranging from 5 G's to Warp Factor 11.

My first school was an urban junior high where many of the students had to cope with economic and social problems along with the standard turmoils of adolescence. Although I truly admired the resilience of the kids in the face of much adversity, I did resent having to pay protection money to certain members of my eighth grade class in order to keep my car intact.

Several years later a move to an affluent suburban setting underscored the universality of youths' unbridled zest for life regardless of living conditions. The change also demonstrated that educators' perceptions of their students' behaviors are shaped by the cocoon in which they work. Whereas in my previous job a fight between students armed with knives was routine, in this new world teachers regarded students speaking loudly in the corridors as a symptom of a serious breakdown in the moral order.

In both schools I also enjoyed the special relationship with students that comes from being a coach, in my case a football coach. From coaching I learned that the VIEW in the locker room (vs. the classroom) is really different — as well as the odor! As an added side job to keep a step ahead of the bill collectors, I also took up private tutoring, which gave me a closer VIEW of students in their homes. Watching kids interact at close quarters with their parents, and more so vice versa, helped me answer numerous burning questions I had about how heredity and environment conspire on the domestic front to make the work of school teachers sometimes delightful but other times agonizing.

Then came a major change. "Look at it this way. Imparting your teaching skills to prospective teachers will enable you to touch the lives of many additional children." These words uttered by the father of one of the turned-off learners I was tutoring, persuaded me to do something I thought would never happen. I left my ideal junior high to become an instructor at a local college. The full impact of my loss soon became apparent. The intimacy of both student and faculty relationships would never be the same. Gone were the students' ski trips and the proms in the gym; finished were the

Friday night faculty poker games and the Saturday morning golf games; vanished were the faculty room jokes and football pools. Yet what fertile vistas were discovered in the billowy stratum of higher (laugh, laugh) learning. Shakespeare's little Puck would have found endless amusement debunking so many of the impostors who have cast themselves into roles as college teachers.

The doctorate, one's ticket required to shed junior status and gain access to the ivory tower, was eventually completed despite the chaos and lunacy of student upheaval sweeping university campuses in the late sixties. It was time to move on once more. The University of Vermont became my Green Mountain professional base from which I ventured out to lead workshops and speak at schools throughout the United States and Canada.

So thirteen years at UVM featured a grueling publish-or-perish climb through tenure to full professorship leading at last to a life of full contentment in the secure ranks of academia, right? Well, not quite. The lure of working on the road, you see, had become very strong. Just as colorful admixtures such as tomato sauce, burgundy wine, brown gravy and mustard are organically prompted to seek out and drip onto snowy white garments, there was the compulsion in me to seek 'perpetual mobility' at all costs: either that or die unfulfilled and embittered. So in 1984 I saw my chance and bade farewell to life as a university professor, despite many hesitant second thoughts. Since then, alas, airports and hotels have become my mobile bases. But the experience has been worth it. Visits to hundreds of schools have added a vast, new dimension to my educational VIEWS. Indeed, what I regarded as a finale has instead proven to be a rich overture.

One common denominator has emerged from all of these experiences. I emphasize it in my presentations again and again, year after year: laughter is tonic for the soul! Maintaining a sense of humor sounds so easy, but for those of you who cope with the realities of school life, laughter can be easily replaced by frowns, cynical mutterings, and the attendant sound of apathy. Do not let it happen to you.

A final thought before you begin. Occasionally someone writes me a vitriolic letter because I have poked fun at their teaching specialty or satirized aspects of their behavior. The writer feels I have maliciously demeaned him or her and educators in general. Nothing could be further from the truth. I am proud of the teaching profession. I respect the academic achievements of my colleagues. I am continually amazed at the dedication the vast majority of educators exhibit and the contributions they make to the lives of students despite the generally negative public scrutiny of education.

Fortunately for me, those who interpret my well intended needling as criticism are few. The overwhelming majority of my audiences appreciate the humor behind the barbs and ribbing. I trust VIEWS will not disappoint them. Enjoy.

CONTENTS

Acknowledgements V

Introduction VII

Chapters

1 The Fastest Scissors in the East 1

2 Management by Eyeball 7

3 Recollection from the Amherst Junior High
School Underground 15

4 The Slow Death of an In-service Instructor 23

5 Confessions of a Chalk Dust Addict 29

6 Alternatives to Educator Strikes 35

7 Answers to Parents' Dumb Questions 41

8 On Being Taken by a Graduate Course 53

9 The Classroom as Theater 59

10 Have Lesson . . . Will Travel 69

11 Coaches' Disease 83

12 The Day I Visited the Gifted and
Talented Classes 89

13 The Lady with the Lickable Face 95

14 A New Source of Guidance Counselor Wisdom 101

15 The Annual Running
of the Schoolhouse Stakes 107

Epilogue 113

1

THE FASTEST SCISSORS
IN THE EAST

Cell 38
Saint Ignatius Monastery
Pawling, New York
August 30
9:00 P.M.

Dear Friend George:
I realize my sudden disappearance has likely caused you and most of my other good friends a fair degree of consternation and has no doubt spawned much speculation as to what actually happened to me. I feel I owe you an explanation so let me put you in the picture. I'll start from the beginning. As you know, Sally and I have been married for 31 years. As we always appeared so happy, I doubt you have any idea what impact her teaching first grade has had on our

married life.

Every year, from the middle of August until late June, I'm competing with projects or competitions in which I generally lose the company of my wife and more. Ever hear of a reading tepee? No? Nor had I, but they exist, and in order to erect such an edifice, many hours of Sally's time and two of my favorite Madras shirts were appropriated. Nor do I know if you have ever heard of a Curiosity Corner. I can only say that in addition to its creation causing me to become a near widower, this activity caused my coin collection, a 27-year endeavor, to be returned to me minus my prized Italian florin. Why, I wonder, don't the parents of my wife's students send in their coin collections for the Curiosity Corner? I don't mean to sound petty, but stuff like this became so pervasive that it just could no longer be overlooked. Something had to give.

Can you blame me? For years I have waited endlessly, patiently, night after night, beginning to think my marriage was weird, causing my behavior to become bizarre. I mean sitting alone in my bedroom wearing a short kimono and feeling amorous gets a little old, not to mention sitting at the top of the stairs playing Italian love songs on my mandolin trying to coax Sal into quitting a little earlier than usual. I mean how would you feel just waiting for the clock to strike 10 then calling down the stairs, "You coming up or what?" and having to endure responses like, "I've got to cut out the pumpkins." Doubtless, you never realized all this. Well it is really something, I can tell you.

As I said, things couldn't continue the way they were going and I considered various responses. First, counter-attack. I could bring home my blueprints and tape them to the walls as she does student drawings and outlines. I could have colleagues calling all hours to ask how my clients are doing. Should I join a bowling league that starts at late hours? I was contemplating such rash actions and worse when I ran into Dave Siegal, the optician, you may know him. He told me about a retreat for spouses of primary teachers which he had attended several years before. You see his wife teaches kindergarten. In short order, I made arrangements and left town within twenty-four hours.

Talk about eye openers! There were forty other spouses of primary teachers from all over the country attending the meetings. My interaction sessions with them have really helped me gain a better perspective on Sally's behavior. For example, I now realize I shouldn't get so mad at her when I return a borrowed tool to a neighbor and upon returning home she inevitably asks, "Did we say thank you?" Or that I shouldn't get livid over her always asking just before we leave on a trip, "Do you have to go to the bathroom before we go bye bye?" Certainly I'm now ashamed at retaliating by coming into our living room holding onto myself as you have seen little boys do, and saying, "I've got to go potty now, bad too." That wasn't very nice, especially in front of Sally's bridge group. I'm also determined that when we're out to dinner and the waiter announces the evening special is roast beef, I'm not going to flip out when Sal widens her eyes and makes gross up and down head movements while saying in that sing-song voice, "Do we want roast beef?" I hope I didn't embarrass you and Ann the night I started blowing bubbles in my water glass after Sally asked me such a question at Antonio's. Or did I start picking my nose? Whatever, forgive me.

Funny, how when one gets down on someone else's behavior, one tends to find fault with just about everything that person does or says. It turns out that Sally's continual complaining about her class last year was more legitimate than I allowed. For example, when she told me she had said to one little hyperactive tyke, "Homer, here's a plastic bag, go play spaceman" I thought, *lady, you're losing it*. However, according to the others in attendance, last year was tough for a lot of their spouses. One woman says her husband got so exasperated trying to teach a first-grader his right hand from his left that he *Krazy Glued* the kid's left hand to the desk so the shaver wouldn't raise it when told to hold up his right hand. Apparently, it didn't help, for when the kid was told to do so, the whole desk became elevated. There's more. A teacher from a district on the tip of Long Island suggested to a troublesome second grade student that he pretend he was Tom Sawyer and build a raft to sail to an island out in the ocean. She further advised him to make it more like the book and not to tell anyone. Fortunately, a fisherman rescued the boy as the raft was heading out to open sea some fifty miles beyond Block Island. Someone has suggested acid rain is the cause of all this craziness; someone else suggested the economy. What do you think?

Rest certain of one thing, George, I'll be returning with a more understanding attitude about Sally's job. No more fighting fire with fire. So what if she doesn't act civilly when she comes through the door after school each day! I flat out refuse any longer to get hostile when my cheery "hello hon" is countered with a gruff, "Will you just please let me go to the toilet, I've been holding it all day!" It must be tough, I finally realize after listening to my friends here, to attend to one's personal needs with the little tykes rattling the doorknob of the classroom toilet while shouting, "Whatcha' doin' in there?" No sir, thanks to Saint Ignatius, I've adopted a much more mellow outlook, perhaps because I have developed a few practical coping skills that can't help but improve matters.

We have had, for example, eight hours of classes in scissors technique. The object being to cut out ducks, numbers, pumpkins, etcetera faster, thus making time for more interesting pursuits — if you follow my drift. In fact, we had a contest and I won the gold scissors trophy by a margin of twelve more ducks cut out than the next closest contestant, a woman from Enid, Oklahoma. We have also had extremely practical intensive tutorials on scissor sharpening and useful seminars on mechanized letter and number cutting devices;

lastly, we have reviewed every available catalog offering free or very inexpensive lessons for use at the primary level. We're all real excited at the prospects for the future of our married lives. After all, a few minutes saved here, a few there, leaves time for, uh, well, you get the picture, right?

I again apologize for leaving without an explanation, but as you have just learned, I had little choice. I'm looking forward to seeing you soon, hopefully, as a changed, much more laid back husband and friend.

Sincerely,

Zach

Alias, The Fastest
Scissors in the East

"Well since you only have six er, uh, balloons, not enough for everyone in class, let's save this for the "show and tell" surprise tomorrow. But show them to your mom and dad and ask if it is all right. Okay Sean?"

2

MANAGEMENT BY EYEBALL

A classroom teacher's key to survival is good discipline. Simple to say, but often quite difficult to achieve. Ask any veteran. Seldom Seated Simon, Totally Talkative Tamara, and Really Rude Robert, not to mention the daily mass uprising at dismissal bell, make this key as difficult to find as advertisements for a meeting of the Urban League Convention in downtown Praetoria. In fact, maintaining sanity in the classroom has made classroom teachers "approaches to discipline" addicts. They just can't get enough Reality Therapy, Logical Consequences or Behavior Mod. Well before you overdose on one or more of these, let me clue you in on the real secret of good classroom management.

Eyes! That is correct, those mirrors of the soul, those silent sentinels of hurt, happiness and lust — peepers, orbs, lamps, oculi — are the key to running a tight ship. To be sure, in the uncultivated state they serve solely to record testimony of ineptness. Trained, however, the eyes become a weapon more disabling than a karate chop, more sobering than a Reverend Moon sermon to airport solicitors who have not met quota, or more attention getting than a politician caught *en flagrante* during an election year.

Fried Egg Gape

There are many different levels of "Management by Eyeball" or *MBE* as I expect it will soon be commonly known. The lowest level, the level requiring the least expertise, is the **Fried Egg Gape**. With comparatively little practice a rank beginner can have some success with this technique. The ultimate **Fried Egg Gape** is achieved by arching the eyebrows while popping out the eyes as far as possible, and at the same time dropping open the mouth until it resembles a yawning chasm. Many individuals are unsure of the description just given so I recommend the following practice techniques. With a full-length mirror positioned before you, leap upon a seatless bicycle. Pay particular attention to the look on your face upon contact. You will behold a perfect **Fried Egg Gape**. A few gifted beginners are able to achieve modest success at this level by observing a top-notch primary teacher in action, but most really proficient educators have had to practice, practice, practice. If no seatless bikes are available, looking in a mirror during a rectal examination by your physician also provides quite similar graphic reproduction of the **Fried Egg Gape** produced with the bicycle training approach. Is it worth it? You will be able to handle most low-level misbehavior with new-found ease, guaranteed!

Cobra Slits

Cobra Slits is the next level in expertise. Here the optimum look is achieved by affecting a grossly sardonic smile, forcing the cheek-bones up while simultaneously pressing the eyebrows downward, creating narrow, snake-like slits out of which your eyes are barely visible. When correctly executed it should be used only in situations where dread terror is required, situations like causing the class clown to *immediately* cease mooning the grandmother who had come to bake class cookies. Warning: this technique requires restraint and any teacher who feels that they might employ it capriciously would be well advised *not* to learn the **Cobra Slits**. Its misuse can cause permanent damage to a student's psyche. Two years ago, for example, a teacher gave a high achiever the **Cobra Slits** for nothing more than asking if she could go to her locker to get her eye visor before a math exam. The teacher admitted later, her deployment of the **Cobra Slits** was grossly over-reactive; small consolation, however, to the parents of the gifted student. The child is still on tranquilizers and according to the deposition filed in their lawsuit, she still wakes up screaming, "Don't let that snake bite me!" Incidentally, using the **Cobra** accompanied by folding your arms and slightly swaying from side to side is devastatingly effective in large group control situations. Why worry about your next cafeteria duty assignment once you have the **Cobra Slits** mastered?

Arch and Close

The **Arch and Close**, or **AC**, is the most subtly devastating weapon in the *MBE* arsenal. This look is simplicity personified; close one eye as though winking, and arch the brow of the other open eye. Universally, this look conveys the message to students, that they have just gone on the teacher's dung list. Executed with proper concentration, this look can get the attention of a student with his back to the teacher! The **AC** is absolutely essential for handling discipline problems during an assembly program where removal of a student creates too much commotion. The power of the **AC** is in its mystery: what is going to happen to me becomes the student's concern rather than acting out.

Double Close

Closely akin to the **AC** is the **DC** or **Double Close**. Used in similar situations as the **AC**, this is the *MBE* technique favored by those teachers who want to rub it in by sending the message, "I'm so powerful I can control without even looking!" It is executed by first gaining the student's attention, then as he or she looks toward the teacher, the teacher simultaneously closes both eyes, flares the nostrils, frowns deeply, and folds arms tightly. A genuine killer. It must be noted that the **AC** and **DC** do not work for many educators, even with practice. This is an *MBE* technique that seems to require some genetic predisposition for success. Those most able to master their use seem to be thin males or females who have a dour personality, thin lips, who use little after-shave lotion or makeup, wear their hair with pomade, straight back or pulled severely back tied in a bun, and would really prefer to be called Professor. Pudgy, perpetually smiling teachers of Greek or Italian heritage who permit students to call them Mr. D or Mrs. G, find that their use of the **AC** or **DC** backfires. Instead of being chastened, students most often convulse with laughter when seeing this teacher's look.

Total Bulge Blast

The ethnic teacher described above must instead use an *MBE* technique that harnesses their jovial personalities, a look that, as contradictory as it sounds, joyfully reprimands. This look is the **Total Bulge Blast**, **TB2** for short. Used in an assembly or to quiet a student who is whispering during another student's oral recitation, the teacher deploys the **TB2** by bulging out the cheeks and eyes (like a maximum **Fried Eggs**) simultaneously. It brings about the desired behavior and at the same time usually evokes a smile from the recipient. As the **AC** or **DC** will backfire when employed by a jovial ethnic, the **TB2** can never be used by those of the dour persuasion mentioned above. Their use of the **TB2** is positively hilarious at best, nauseating at worst.

Warning: Of all *MBE* techniques, the **AC** and **DC** evoke the strongest student reactions when subjected to them. Students have often been observed muttering obscenities, making finger gestures, or writing rather unflattering graffiti about the teacher on lavatory walls and doors. Use the **AC** and **DC** infrequently and balance their use with positive strokes or run the risk of having your tires slashed or worse. Do not let the narcotic feeling of power the **AC** or **DC** encourages lure you under its spell. Kids do not mind being called when it is deserved, but over-using the sardonic black widow thing is asking for trouble.

Fried Egg Gape — Thunder Ray Finger Combo

This brings us to the highest level of *MBE*, also the most difficult, the **Fried Egg Gape—Thunder Ray Finger Combo**. Think it is hard to say, trying to perform it is infinitely more difficult, requiring years of supervised practice under the tutelage of a master. The difficulty is due to the incredible precision necessary to make the **Combo** work. Without this precision the technique can backfire on the user and create a worse classroom management problem than the one confronted initially. Greatly simplified, the **Combo** employs a **Fried Egg Gape** which, at its dramatic zenith, is augmented by a rigid point of the index finger while simultaneously snapping the fingers loudly, deafeningly! All three moves occur simultaneously, in absolute precision. How difficult is this precision? Experts liken it to the combined routines of Nureyev and Fonteyn in their prime!

Results, however, are commensurate with the effort required for mastery. Documented cases exist that indicate miscreants have been physically stunned by the **Combo**, several actually driven to their knees. Students have reported soiling their underclothes routinely when nailed with the **Combo**. Debriefed after one such incident, the student reported, "It was as though I was being bombarded by an invisible ray coming from the teacher's eyes and finger." The badly shaken student concluded, "I was really scared."

Now comes the hitch. There are so few **Combo** masters still teaching, let alone willing to take on apprentices, there exists a genuine fear the technique may become a lost art. Despite this somber note, those determined to gain mastery of the **Combo** can take heart. There are a few **Combo** masters about but not many teachers know where to look. If you are dead serious and willing to commit yourself to the quest and work like a dog, locate a top notch, academically oriented parochial private school where the nuns still wear the old style habits and say their mass in Latin. If, for example, you find this is a place where they play guitars at mass, this is not the place you should seek the **Combo** master. When you do find this person who will undoubtedly be quite elderly, prostrate yourself at her feet and tell her of your desire. If you are one of the fortunate ones, she will accept you as an apprentice. Be warned, however, mastery is not by any means guaranteed.

In conclusion I realize that doubters and cynics, legion in our profession, will likely ridicule *MBE* as but another gimmick. So be it. But to all such doubters I make one request to illustrate the potential power of the eyes: take a hard look at a portrait of George Patton, Wyatt Earp, or most of all the Ayatollah Khomeini. Particularly study their eyes. I'm certain that will make you at least willing to consider eye power.

"*God, please let it be closed. It's been such a long stretch since Christmas and Easter is still three plus weeks away. My pupils need a break too you know, Lord.*"

3

RECOLLECTION FROM THE AMHERST JUNIOR HIGH SCHOOL UNDERGROUND

I came into teaching with stars in my eyes. Profs who wrote placement file recs used descriptive terms like "idealistic," "enthusiastic," and "full of energy." My own self-perceptions were far from immodest: I intended to change the world, period! All that remained was to find the right school in which to make my mark. I decided on a suburban junior high school called Amherst. Now the task was to get hired. I'd been around enough to know that if you did a good job and kept your nose clean, you would likely be on the right side of the boss, the building principal. The principal? Was I out to lunch on that one. To be sure, the principal who interviewed me and I *thought* hired me, certainly acted like the boss. During the interview he asked all the right questions: what was my philosophy of education; what were the keys to good classroom management; what was my attitude toward standardized testing and so forth. Hey, I was completely taken in; this person was obviously the man.

I should have picked up my first clue as to what was really up when the principal took me on a tour of the building. Think about it: we spent no more than five minutes with my future department head, three or four in the faculty room, and over two hours with Herbie, the man whom I came to call the Godfather, the head custodian. We didn't meet in his regular office either. Oh no, we met in his very private and spacious office two levels below the main floor, an office located behind the two huge boilers that serviced the entire building. Herbie's questions seemed innocuous at the time: Enjoy playing poker? Are you a sloppy teacher? Were you from a home where parents gave you everything? Mind you, all of this was asked in a very low key manner but there was no mistaking the fact that he was listening very carefully to my answers, which I could tell he liked. And though it didn't register then, as the principal and I were leaving, out of the corner of my eye I saw Herbie make a thumbs-up sign. How could I possibly have known that meant I was hired, *regardless* of what anyone else thought . . . including the principal and superintendent?

There were three of us hired that year. Joyce, a hotshot science teacher who was also a hotshot eater, and looked it; Tommie, an ex-Marine who taught social studies and coached track; and me, for English and coaching football. Had we compared notes after the first orientation meeting, perhaps a clue to the power structure would have emerged. It may have struck them odd as it did me, that the person who had the longest presentation was not the superintendent or the board chairman or the union president, but Herbie, who by the way was also district chief custodian. Get this, when Herbie was introduced everyone rose and gave him a standing ovation. I mean we're talking a stomping, whistling, hooting, cheering stand "O". The loudest cheers came from a veteran guidance counselor named Burt Adams whom I later discovered was touted to be the heir apparent to the superintendent's job when the present super retired. Get the picture? I didn't then, but I do now.

Herbie not only reviewed building improvements made over the summer but also went through a step-by-step demonstration of how rooms were to be left after each school day, prior to a teacher leaving, you know, shade levels, lights off, etc. All the veterans in the room nodded as one as each point was made. Again, when he finished, the entire throng rose in applauding tribute . . . all except poor Joyce. I think it was just too much of an effort for her weight-wise. I also think that signaled the beginning of the end for her. You see, she never returned from Christmas recess. Fired. Too bad she sat in the first row at that orientation meeting. Both Adams and Herbie saw her not stand the second time.

Ah, those glorious autumn days of October and November. As they passed I began to feel really good about the school, my peers, the students and the job in general. I felt I was doing a good job, but hardly worthy of the praise I received. I was singled out for compliments by everyone from the superintendent and board president on down, praise both public and private. I guess I was so busy feeling self-satisfied that I never put two and two together. The truth was my exceedingly positive press was not attributable to outstanding pedagogy or talent but because Herbie liked me, really liked me. Though I was at five-seven, four inches taller than he, he nicknamed me the "Little Fella," a name by which everyone in the administration and, of course, Adams, referred to me. Some people thought I should be offended by the name but I took it in stride. Who cared? I was the only faculty member with a standing invitation to the boiler room for coffee and doughnuts anytime I cared to come, which was every day. I liked being with those guys as the conversation was always easy, and sports or sex dominated the topics. It wasn't long before I began to realize Herbie was taking me into his confidence, sharing his feelings about school issues and other staff members. He didn't do it maliciously, just sort of casually mentioned his observations concerning the world about us. From day one Joyce was at the top of his dung list: didn't straighten up her room, left boards unerased, lights on, and sin of sins, left a window open. Thank God I never really got to know her well. As I mentioned earlier, she never came back from Christmas recess, just disappeared without a trace.

Another person who came in for regular blasts was a veteran teacher named Troy Hardison, a math instructor. He too never erased his boards. "What's wrong with his arm, broken?" Herbie would rail. The Herbie-Hardison tension grew and after the fourth subtle hint by the principal concerning the boards, Hardison was told on a Friday that the following Monday he would be teaching his classes in a converted storeroom that was dark, stuffy and totally inadequate. The explanation for the change was that the head custodian determined his regular room needed immediate emergency maintenance work. Hardison protested to the administration, board and parents. No change. I discreetly suggested to Troy, when his protests brought no relief, that he cop a plea with Herbie and apologize for past transgressions and promise to keep his boards clean. He reluctantly did so and within a week he was back in his room. Reflecting back on it, I believe this was the incident which gave me my first inkling as to what was really going on concerning the power structure in the district. Not a real awareness, just a feeling, you understand.

Why didn't I fully comprehend you might ask? I wasn't a rube who hadn't been around or something like that. I've concluded in retrospect that the reason was I was just getting along so well I didn't have to concern myself with Machiavellian stratagems. Yet, subconsciously I was involved in power brokering intrigues. Let me explain. I remember telling Herbie I wanted to go to a national meeting at district expense, a no-no according to the grapevine. He suggested I put in my request quietly without noising it around the faculty room. Fully expecting a big fat "who do you think you are?" answer from the principal, guess what I got? "I'm really glad you asked and, of course, we would be happy to support the trip but let's keep it confidential." On another occasion I mentioned to Herbie I wanted to put in for the reading position, a job regarded as a plum, but I was reluctant since I knew several other more senior faculty were also interested. He encouraged me to apply anyway, noting that one never knows what can happen. I got the appointment.

Well, Herbie's advice only helped you, you're thinking. No way. I downplayed my personal successes and before long other people began seeking my input on problems or questions of some concern to them, particularly about requests or petitions they were planning to make to the administration. I wasn't consciously aware of how I reacted but what I invariably did was, over coffee, mention what I had been told and then I just listened to what Herbie had to say on the matter. I then took what he, casually mind you, opined and made this the gist of what I would suggest as advice to the person who had sought my counsel. In every instance, those guided by my counsel seemed to prosper, those who ignored it failed. Take, for example, Alice McGill, the Home Ec teacher — Tight Wad McGill to Herbie — so-called because she never even presented Herbie or any of his crew a five-pack of cigars on Christmas. She ignored my advice not to ask for an extra couple of days off following the Christmas recess. Despite the fact she was willing to take the days as unpaid leave, she was turned down flat and told she would be fired if she took the time anyway. Then there was Gus Casper, the Driver's Ed guy who kept parking too close to the fuel oil fill pipe, a cardinal transgression according to Herbie. Casper asked me how to approach the administration about using a school van to take his students to a driving rodeo in Massachusetts. After my usual *consultation* procedure, I told him I doubted the idea would get to first base — and it didn't. Realizing this was also a big blow to his students, I strongly suggested he not park near the oil fill and to make peace with Herbie, which he did. Herbie, ever magnanimous, accepted the apology. . .with a little priming from yours truly. To whit: after resubmitting his request, Casper's group not only got the school van for their trip but have been to practically every national rodeo since. Now you tell me, coincidence? There is a P.S. to this story, by the way. Two years ago our Driver's Ed team won the national competition. A campaign was launched to award Casper a new car as a token of the school's affection and pride. The Aldermanic Council, the School Board, and most importantly, the mayor were all adamantly opposed to such a gift; Herbie was four square behind the idea. What chance would a custodian have against the power elite of the city? Casper got the car, the mayor got canned. I think I made my point.

And so it went over the years. Fortunately for me, Herbie retired just four years ago. He was almost seventy-five, ten years beyond what was supposed to be the *mandatory* age for retirement. I retire this June. I've continued to visit Herbie and have our little coffee klatsch conversations. Has he lost his clout? You decide. When the district superintendent retired, two hotshot Doctorates from out of town applied for the position; one of these candidates had even been a Rhodes Scholar. The school board was rumored to be unanimously backing the hiring of someone outside the district, citing the need for new perspectives. Herbie, during one of my visits to his home, told me Adams was still the best man for the job. I thought, *Herbie's out-of-step on this one for sure*. Our new superintendent was named last Thursday night. Burt Adams.

I'm sure that young pre-service novices contemplating a career in education think me an old school fuddy-duddy when I tell them of all the advice to heed, none is more important than this old educational bromide: your building custodian can make or break you. They never say it but I know they think this is the stupidest piece of advice we've ever been given. All I'll say in closing is remember, in education some things always change yet stay the same.

© Zach Clements, 1990

"Big deal. Doctorate from Harvard, Rhodes Scholar. I'm telling you now just like I told you before, I'm not voting for anyone to fill the superintendency vacancy who hasn't been an athletic director, period!"

4

THE SLOW DEATH OF AN IN-SERVICE INSTRUCTOR

"Pardon," I asked yet again. Never having been an accomplished lip reader, so far over did I lean toward the tiny lady I sensed was speaking to me, my ear was practically in her mouth. She was speaking and as I had surmised, directing her comment to me.

"Since you are the university expert doing our in-service course, perhaps you might consent to visit my seventh period class to help me determine why the students are so listless and disinterested in biology. I've never encountered a group like them in all my years."

"I don't know about being an expert, but I certainly would be happy to observe and offer some suggestions that might be of help," I fairly screamed, assuming she was having as much trouble hearing me as I her. "Would you like me to come to tomorrow's seventh period class, that's at 2:26, right?"

After bending to retrieve her glasses which I had fairly blown from her face, she sheepishly replied, "I think that would be fine. See you then." She quickly disappeared out the door doubtless relieved she would not have to endure another vocal typhoon.

Following her departure, despite my exasperation over communicating with an individual one degree short of being mute, I was rather delighted when several other faculty who had overheard her request told me I should be quite flattered, as Mrs. Hoose, a wily veteran, was not one to lightly admit to having disinterested students. It seemed I had achieved a breakthrough of sorts. All agreed any assistance I could render her would be a bona fide feather in my cap. So what if I had to resort to signing, giving hand signals. Rule number one of any workshopper: be prepared to overcome any obstacle thrown in your path. Rule number two: never arrive late for an observation. I was late.

I was delayed in the line of duty, however. I had to stop to console a tearful seventh grader who it seems had lost a sneaker he was wearing. Apparently, while hurrying from the gym to his next class, the poor creature suddenly noticed that one of the sneakers he had been wearing was no longer on his foot. "I had them both on when I left the gym and when I looked down one was gone, right Steve?" sobbed the semi-shoeless Joe Jackson. His friend nodded agreement while maintaining an appropriately moribund countenance. "My mother is going to kill me," concluded the unfortunate boy who had suffered this ignominious loss. Fortunately, the assistant principal appeared on the scene and took charge of the missing sneaker caper. Small consolation as I was now five minutes late for my rendezvous with my feathered cap.

Arriving at the door, I pushed it open slowly and entered as silently as possible, taking care not to even allow the door latch to click as it closed. As I started tiptoeing toward the rear, down the aisle between the first and second rows, Mrs. Hoose briefly halted her lesson and gave me a nod of greeting, her eyes flicking a glance up at the clock; I pretended not to notice. As I made my way down the aisle a strange thing happened. Each student I passed reached out to me in a manner reminiscent of what I had witnessed in the central bazaar of Marakesh, only now instead of the words, "Alms," these beggars' hoarse pleadings consisted of one word repeated over and over, "Wahhhter, wahhhter." I literally had to use short karate chops to prevent clutching fingers from impeding my progress. I was appalled at the swollen lips and sorrowful pleading eyes I beheld and thus felt greatly relieved at finally reaching my place at the back of the room.

As I gazed about the classroom more bizarre sights caught my attention. Every plant, recall this was a biology class, was limp. The inhabitants of the aquarium were absolutely immobile, a strange behavior I thought until I closely examined the thermometer in the water; it read 170°. The fish were in the process of being poached! I looked over at the cage which housed the white mice and almost jumped out of my skin when I realized the one mouse moving slowly about the cage was not making random movements but was etching in the sand the last letter of a word, a word that spelled, let me see, W-A-T-E-R, water, that was the word. *What is this*, I thought to myself, *a Stephen King movie set or something?* I looked around fully expecting to see the lens of a hidden camera protruding from an air vent or light fixture. Maybe it was a Candid Camera episode? No such luck. This was reality. It was really happening.

I tried to see what Mrs. Hoose was writing on the board, but could not make it out due to the shimmering heat waves. As she mumbled something about molecular cohesion, Thud!, the sound of a collapsing student's head hitting a desk was heard. Thud! Thud, Thud! Three more were down. A young female student appeared to literally melt from her seat onto the floor. Shocked by what I was observing I made up my mind to throw caution to the winds and rush over to the windows and fling them all open. But what's this? My legs would not work. That's when it hit me: I was in the initial stages of dehydration collapse. I was having trouble focusing my vision and my thought process was becoming confused and disjointed. I also came to the realization **I** was mumbling the word "wahhter." I knew one thing, panic had to be avoided. To curb hyperventilation I began to breathe slowly and deeply, concentrating on but one goal, do not pass out. Cardinal rule of all workshopper rules: do not pass out during an observation.

I am not sure whether I beheld a mirage, but what else could the burnoose clad student that raised his hand and responded to a question possibly have been? Months later, I was still unsure this mirage really happened. I began praying for a miracle when I discovered the lead in my pencil had attained the consistency of soft putty. *Oh, why did I ever leave the security of my own public school classroom? Oh God, get me through this and I promise I'll never do another in-service workshop as long as I live*, were my thoughts. Pathetic, eh?

God must have been listening because Mrs. Hoose walked over to the windows and while a voice in my head screamed, *Open it, Open it, I will you to open the window*. She did, about three inches. The cool moist air, literally a draught of life, seemed to revive at least half the class and me. Mrs. Hoose, however, though wearing a wool dress and sweater, proceeded to take her heavy fur trimmed coat from the closet prior to resuming the lesson. "I hope that makes you all happy now that I'm freezing to death" was her observation on the life saving ventilation gesture.

BRRRRRIIIINNNNG! The bell signaling the end of the hour had a Pavlovian effect on the entire class. Students, moments before on the verge of heat prostration, leaped from their seats and quickly hurried out the door whereupon they

literally streaked to the water fountain, each drinking greed-
ily while enduring the curses and threats of those still await-
ing their turns.

"Now do you see what I mean about their listless behavior
and total disinterest," Mrs. Hoose asked me as soon as the last
student had departed the room. "I declare it is because they
are up all hours of the night watching television. What do you
recommend? Lowering grades?"

"No," I replied.

"More exams?"

"No."

"Demand the school give these students physicals?"

"No."

"Well, what in heavens name do you suggest, Mr. Workshop Expert?" finally shouted an obviously exasperated
Mrs. Hoose.

"Canteens," I literally screamed.

Postscript

This episode occurred six months ago. I do not know
whether my suggestion was even accepted, let alone whether
it worked or not. I have not been back in that building since
that day. I do not even remember leaving the room, but
apparently I did and was found six hours later wandering on
the outskirts of town. Those who found me report I was
delirious, incoherent, and babbling senselessly. Needless to
say, I am no longer doing in-service workshops. I just hope one
day to be able to once again achieve gainful employment.
They tell me Mrs. Hoose has decided not to retire for at least
one more year. I guess her new-found notoriety status
affected her decision. It seems that an unprecedented number
of her students, sixteen of them in fact, have been accepted for

Peace Corps hardship placements in Third World posts near the Sahara and Gobi. Further, rumor has it that these students completed their training in one-third the time normally required.

"Isn't that something," remarked the fellow who was sharing this information with me at the convalescent home where he had come to visit, "Eh, Zach?"

I could not answer. His comments had evoked a traumatic reaction, a vivid flashback. I again beheld the burnoose clad, notebook toting student, only this time he was astride a camel.

* * * *

The Gospel According to Mark . . . a Kindergartner

Once, while visiting a kindergarten at a parochial school in New Jersey, I witnessed a delightful interpretation of Scriptures that only a kindergartner could create. "Well, what did you learn from today's Bible story, Mark?" asked Sister Eileen. The freckled-faced red headed boy thought for a moment and replied, "I think it was about many were cold and few were frozen." Seeing the look of dismay on Sister Eileen's face, he quickly added, "But don't worry, Sister, 'cause God will make them all warm."

5

CONFESSIONS OF A CHALK DUST ADDICT

Prefatory Remarks

Oh, how I pine for a time past when the term substance abuse meant taking a furtive drag on a parent's not quite crushed butt or more likely, imagining doing it, then using embellished bravado to describe the incident. Oh, for a time past when there were cultural taboos shrouded in delicious mystery that fired the imagination of all adolescents. Oh, for the time when, according to the *Boy Scout Manual*, "hair growth on the palms and a sallow complexion" were undisputable outcomes of reckless impetuosity of youth. Oh, for a time when the reckless abandonment of youth could be later recalled with mirth and wonderment at our sweet naiveté. Come, share the laughter of one such recollection.

* * * *

I did my first chalk dust, **CD** as the cognoscente called it, when I was ten, in Mrs. Wolfson's class at Ferris Avenue Elementary. I'm sure peer pressure had a lot to do with it. Why am I saying this when I'm not sure that peers should be blamed? Did we even have peer pressure in 1943? Up to that time I had only picked up hints about stuff like that from the big guys in the neighborhood: Bananas Delfino, Zookie Zanazzi and Bang-Bang Zilembo. I'm sure the thrill of the unknown was a factor, subconsciously anyway. Because I have to admit their tales, lurid tales of clapping erasers behind the school, fired my imagination, especially when they would talk of passing the "e's" around and getting "one more big hit" out of what looked like a "thoroughly clean one." If that's peer pressure then it had something to do with it, but I don't think so.

You see, this was exciting talk but also frightening. It was common knowledge one could get hooked on CD and become an addict like my cousin Bananas had during that very school year. Plus, I'm sure all their talk was mainly bravado because in order for what they were saying to be true, the teachers had to be involved, and I just couldn't imagine that. But Bananas made me change my mind. Poor Bananas. Every time I saw him after school he evinced the telltale signs: faint yellow powder stains, not only on his arms and clothes, but in his hair and around his mouth and nose. His eyes were always red and irritated. It must have begun to affect his brain as well because when anyone asked him a question, like why he was so late, he'd just stretch out his arms, then slowly bring his hands together, repeating the motion over and over. Imagine a guy doing an eraser clapping imitation right out in the street . . . in broad daylight! The guy was either gutsy or really gonzoed, more likely gonzoed. It didn't take long for people to begin whispering about his apparent problem and it wasn't long before he began losing tips because his customers were getting peeved about having him deliver their newspapers so late. But the guy seemed completely oblivious to the fact that CD was turning his wallet into a sieve.

"Bananas," I asked him one day, "why are you delivering the papers so late and stuff like that?" I avoided actually using the term "clapping" or "CD" because he was pretty tough and how was I to know whether or not the stuff had messed up his brain sufficiently that he might be prone to violence, cousin or no cousin.

"Heh, heh, heh," was his reply, that same funny chuckle I heard his brother Coco call a "horny snicker." I never quite got the drift of that remark because Bananas played drums, not a horn. The laugh and the far-off look, you know, glassy, coupled with the way he licked his lips gave me my answer: he was hooked! I vowed never to let this happen to me. Never!

Never turned out to be about a month. On a beautiful lilac-scented May afternoon Mrs. Wolfson approached me and asked me — no, whispered to me — "Would you like to stay after school to clean the erasers?" To this day I don't know what made me agree. I am sure the Devil was involved because I had skipped church the previous Sunday to go fishing, or maybe Satan was in on things because I laughed when I saw a hole in Father Geralimo's shoe sole when he genuflected at the altar while I was serving as altar boy that month. Whatever, I nodded okay to Mrs. Wolfson. Later, as the last of the class shuffled out the door, I could feel my pulse quickening. I actually felt faint. What had I done? In a few minutes I would be exposing myself to chalk dust. Intentionally! I didn't want to become another Bananas. Maybe I could tell Mrs. Wolfson I was sick or pretend to vomit. My mind was racing, filled with bizarre escape scenarios.

"All right, Zacharie, you can erase the boards now, then take the erasers out," Mrs. Wolfson called to me, at the same time gesturing toward the front boards filled with writing and arithmetic problems . . . lots of chalk!

So it was true. The teachers were involved. If I walked any slower toward the board I would not have been moving at all.

"Hurry along now," she said. "We would both like to get home soon, I'm sure."

Sure, what's it matter to you, I thought, *I notice you aren't risking getting hooked.* I was glad she turned her attention to the bulletin board that ran along the left side of the room where Ducky Censullo and Moose sat. Perhaps now she wouldn't notice the sweat forming on my forehead, not only a result of my feelings of dread, but also from trying to hold my breath so not to inhale the chalk dust generated by the erasing process. I was moving the eraser ever so slowly, trying to keep the dust to an absolute minimum. Finally, after what seemed an eternity, the last of the yellow scrawls were reduced to faint smudges. Only then did I permit myself to take a breath.

"I'm going outside now," I called to Mrs. Wolfson, whose sole acknowledgement was a wave of her arm, her back still to me as she concentrated on the bulletin board task. I knew the corner of the building where it was rumored Bananas and the others did their clapping but I wasn't going over to that dark closed-in space. I knew for sure you'd get a full snort without even trying. I decided to stand along the west wall near the office windows and reach around the corner to clap the eraser against the north wall, the one with no windows. That way, I reasoned, I would not get dusted. My plan was working to perfection. Six of my eight erasers were clapped clean and I hadn't gotten the slightest whiff of CD. I now knew only weaklings had to sniff CD, while a guy with some backbone could do clapping without succumbing to getting dusted!

Doubtless emboldened by my newly discovered self-discipline, I went at the last two erasers with reckless abandon, smiting the most soiled of them with most thunderous thwacks, when the wind blew a huge cloud of yellow powder into my face. I wheezed and coughed furiously, attempting to expel the fine particles I could now taste, let alone smell and feel burning my eyes. I was instantly aware of the futility of my efforts. I had to face the fact that, inadvertently to be sure, I had done CD! I was alarmed to the extent that I didn't try to clean the last eraser at all. As I hurried around the building toward the entrance near my classroom, I carefully reconnoitered the area. As far as I could tell, no one had witnessed my act. What a break!

A break? Beholding my reflection in a windowpane sobered me like a stinging slap. The telltale signs were all too evident: yellow dust in my T-zone area, in my hair, and worse, yellow stains between my fingers. My mind was crazy with panic. Still, a plan began to formulate in my head. If I went home the back way, along the tracks, I could slip into the house and wash up before any of the neighbors or my grandmother saw me. That's what I would do. I couldn't wait to get rid of these lousy erasers and get out of school. I returned to the classroom to find the door was locked and the lights were out. Maybe Mrs. Wolfson was in the teachers' room. As I silently crept down the intermediate wing toward the teachers' lounge, I actually began to feel a little afraid. The building seemed so strange and large now that it was deserted. Paranoia! Was I already experiencing a symptom of CD use? Was I going on a bad trip my first time? I had never been to the teachers' room. What do I do? Knock? Walk in? Call out? As I approached the door, I noticed the curtain that normally completely covered the small window in the door was partially opened, enabling me to peek in.

No Mrs. Wolfson was in sight. Bananas' teacher, Miss Jervis, a young blond from California, was sprawled on a large couch, her skirt pushed up so high I could see the tops of her stockings and the garters holding them up. Opposite her sat the attractive black-haired college girl who was her student teacher. The student teacher was brushing her hair. The rapid arm movement caused her front to bounce and jiggle. A rush! The funny feeling that came over me was no doubt a CD rush I'd heard about. It was like a warm, almost hot glowing feeling in my gut and at the nape of my neck. It was a wonderful feeling like nothing I had ever felt before. I was floating!

I slowly backed away from the door and made my way back to my classroom where I left the erasers piled outside the locked door. As I hurried home along the railroad tracks, I became aware of a stark reality. A chalk dust high was really fantastic! I also realized I'd be doing erasers a lot. Maybe I was hooked, but what a terrific feeling.

That night I bumped into Bananas. He must have caught on immediately, despite the fact that I had made certain not a speck of yellow was on me, because without any hesitation he came right out and asked, "So, how did you like it, Cuz?" A knowing smile spread across his face.

My reply: "Heh, heh, heh."

6

ALTERNATIVES TO EDUCATOR STRIKES

The recent amalgamation of the Minnesota Teachers Federation and the Brotherhood of Cement Packers and Olive Grove Workers International based in New York City and Palermo, Italy has provoked much discussion in labor, education and government circles. The following is an exclusive *Education Review* interview with P. Vincenzo (Three Fingers) Massonelli, Executive Director of the newly merged unions and a model for one of the characters in the book *The Gang That Couldn't Shoot Straight*. The interview was conducted at BCPOGWI Headquarters in Palermo, Sicily.

ER: Mr. Massonelli, can you tell us what major educational issues are confronting the BCPOGWI and how your union plans to address these issues with what you have been quoted as saying are alternatives to traditional educator strikes?

VM: As you are aware, educator strikes have for the most part been counterproductive when compared to the results of a work stoppage in our sector. Our new members, therefore, are looking to us for more effective approaches to having legitimate concerns addressed. Let me discuss these concerns and our innovative plans for creating public awareness and support for those issues.

Walking about carrying a sign that reads "**NO DISCIPLINE — NO TEACHING**" can't compare to our positive attention getting devices. In each school where student misbehavior is a problem, teachers conduct a secret meeting to identify the individual students who are most disruptive. On an appointed night, five burly faculty members in a stolen car abduct two or three of these students chosen at random from the master hit list. The abductees are summarily tarred and feathered and dropped in front of the local television station. Subsequently, instructions are received from an anonymous caller: broadcast a taped message found in an abandoned car near the town park. The message:

No longer will educators of the area be subjected
to student abuse or tolerate student misbehavior.
This is the first of a series of punishments
scheduled to be meted out to those who do not
follow the rules. Parents and your children,
consider yourselves forewarned!

—The Lovers of Education Brigade

As with public apathy concerning internecine gang feuds and murders, I suspect the authorities will make a lukewarm investigation. More importantly, instead of the enmity that strikes usually create, citizens are likely to applaud, except those, of course, involved in tar removal.

ER: Well, certainly that is an alternative approach, Mr. Massonelli. What are some of your other concerns?

VM: The public is so used to hearing educators crying poverty, that the picket signs asking for more money are meaningless. I propose a kamikaze approach, a few sacrificing all for the many. After an emotional address by the union, er, association leaders, as many of these education unionists insist on being called, highlighting the injustice of denied salary demands, an appeal is made for two volunteers from each building. If the oratorical skills of the speakers have been sufficiently persuasive, volunteers should not be hard to recruit. We have never had trouble finding zealous people among the cement or olive labor force.

Over a period of several weeks, these recruits are thoroughly brainwashed concerning the justice of their cause. When their zeal is at its peak each is issued a Saturday Night Special and instructed to hold up a blind newsstand operator or a mom and pop grocery . . . and get caught. Undoubtedly, during arraignment when the profession of these *criminals* becomes known, great media attention will be attracted. Once before the cameras and microphones, our heroes pour out a tale of financial woe and personal family deprivation that drove them to their dastardly crime for which they are now sorely repentant. If this confession is properly done, much public sympathy will surely be engendered, far more than would have accrued from a strike. Of concern, certainly, is the fate of the volunteers. It is unlikely they will ever be employed in a school again, and though judges will likely suspend their sentences, there will be some stigma attached to their actions.

The association must elevate these individuals to hero status on the local and national levels while providing them with a salary equal to what they would have been earning. The association will most likely want to hire these people to train future kamikazes. We are also toying with the idea of trying to recruit volunteers with a literary bent. That way, in the event they don't get a suspended sentence, they can use their time inside writing their memoirs which the union can publish and then earn income from the sales.

ER: Sounds very interesting and unique. You've been very vocal about parents' lack of involvement with schools. Can you elaborate on this matter and how it relates to strikes?

VM: Here is a more realistic approach. Parents who refuse to cooperate with teachers and school officials, never coming to meetings, ignoring requests for conferences, are a legitimate concern of educators. But does carrying a sign saying "**PARENTS UNCOOPERATIVE**" really have a chance at changing things for the better? No. I propose this: once faculty polls indicate which parents are most uncooperative, a faculty member with contacts in the Ma. . . I mean our educational council, meets with a representative of the organization and negotiates on behalf of the faculty a price for calling on the recalcitrant parents to "make them an offer they can't refuse." The costs to an association for this persuasive service will be considerably less than a strike, except where a car or two has to be burned — even more expensive if the occupants are still in it — to get the more stubborn parents to respond. Despite these few complications that will undoubtedly be the exceptions, I can guarantee far greater parent cooperation than ever dreamed.

ER: I don't mean to be disrespectful, but most educators are familiar with organizations like the Elks, League of Women Voters and the Odd Fellows. They know very little about meeting a representative of the organization to which you refer. How would they proceed?

VM: This is why the uniting of our two groups, the teachers with the cement packers and olive workers, makes such good sense. I realize that educators in places like Cylinder, Iowa or Poplar, Montana would have a hard time making the appropriate contacts. But now all any of these locals have to do is contact me and I'll fix everything. Capisco, huh? [winks and summons a consigliere to his side.]

"You see Don Rococo, I'm a principal. I've got these two teachers who hate kids but I can't get them to resign, so I was hoping..."

7

ANSWERS TO PARENTS' DUMB QUESTIONS

Y es, kids say the darndest things. But as a teacher of many years, I have also learned that parents ask the darndest questions, often at the most inconvenient or inopportune times. Query anyone who has been in teaching for more than a year or two — especially at the elementary level — as to what irritates them more than any other aspect of their job, they will likely respond: "Answering the stupid questions parents ask — year after year after year!" It is almost as though the first day mommas and poppas enroll their offspring they magically obtain a manual of inane inquiries to which some miscreant dedicated to the derangement of teachers keeps adding new entries.

Hemorrhoids, ulcers and varicose veins are all taken for granted as occupational hazards, but the ability to remain nonplussed in the face of these perennial insipid interrogations tests the metal of even the most professional educators. But I guess they aren't building us the way they used to because my metal seems to be corroding and, as a result, I have decided to go on the offensive. The next time I am asked something like "how come you don't teach Latin in the elementary anymore?" I am going to zap the questioner with a comeback that will have Don Rickles seeking my services as a writer.

Below are but a tantalizing sample of the gems I intend to use in reply to parents who have the temerity to ask me a dumb question. Each is vintage, having been mellowing (or is it stewing?) over a good many years. My plan of attack is simplicity personified: upon hearing the question I shall reply in a calm, conversational tone of voice in no way betraying the inner hostility I feel toward my antagonist. I invite you to use any or all but suggest you be aware of one important prerequisite: know where you will be employed next!

The Missing Mitten Inquiry

I'm sitting home in my living room/study where I have just cut out 32 valentine patterns, corrected innumerable work sheets, planned next week's lessons and filled in 26 progress reports. I'm tired — no, exhausted, contemplating a hot bath, a bit of light reading when . . . ring-a-ling goes the phone . . .

I : Hello, Zach Clements here.

Parent: This is Mrs. Green, Kimberley's mother, calling. I'm sorry to bother you but I'm pretty upset about something and decided to give you a call, even though it's late.

I : Well, I'm sorry about that. How can I help?

Parent: Kim came home today with one mitten missing. Now I've already purchased her two new pairs this school year to replace mittens she has lost. What in heaven's name are **YOU** doing with them?

I : I **EAT** them, what else? When the kids aren't looking I sneak over to their cubbies and take just one mitten out of two or three, depending on what I'm cooking that evening. I love to stew them in chicken broth spiced with garlic, oregano and bay leaves. Sliced and served with hot pepper and anchovies, they make a great antipasto. You should try it. It is going to be all the rage in haute eateries, and very soon.

The Harboring Cutthroat Investigation

I've said Happy Chanukah and Merry Christmas so many times that I'm almost hoarse, but now the last of kids have screamed out the door and I finally start to relax. The euphoric thought of ten days to gird myself for the long haul till Easter almost makes me dizzy. "Mr. Clements," the office intercom blasts, "telephone call at the office."

I : (wearily) Hello, this is Mr. Clements.

Parent: Mr. Clements, this is Rev. Spiedecker, Malcolm's father, calling. Last night Malcolm revealed something at dinner that has caused Mrs. Spiedecker and me a great deal of anxiety. It seems that one of his fellow second grader's brought a knife to school and actually showed it to Malcolm. Malcolm said that he reported it but you allowed the boy to keep it, provided he didn't take it out again. Do you encourage children to bring dangerous weapons to school?

I : Well, I was actually angry because Jimmy didn't follow my instructions. I told him to bring a pistol or, at a minimum, a sword. However, it seems that all he could find was that foolish mini inch-and-a-half nail clipper; he found it in a *Cracker Jack* box. Rest assured that, unless he brings something more awesome than that, I don't intend to use him in my shakedown operation I'm planning to start in the primary lavatories. You tip off Mally-babe that if he wants in he'd better locate at least a 22-caliber zip gun or forget it. What's that? You're going to take this up with the authorities. Go ahead . . . and make my day!

The Roots Ruckus

I am almost in tears as I read a letter of thanks from a Thai parent who recently left our district. She was commending me and my class on how wonderfully we accepted her son who came to our class only two weeks after arriving in America; the kids really had taken him under their collective wings. The office switchboard operator calls the faculty room to tell me the mother of one of my students would like to talk with me. I suggest she meet me in my classroom where we can have some privacy. I excuse myself and hurry down to tidy up the place.

I : Oh, hello Mrs. White, just tidying up a bit.

Parent: Good afternoon, Mr. Clements, or is it really ClementEE, but no matter. Let me get right to the point. Both my husband and I are a little concerned about what I'll call, for want of a better term, your apparent preoccupation with ethnicity relating to your students and as son William says you refer to it — your own "Italianness." Though my heritage goes back to the *Mayflower*, in no way do I consider myself against those who just got off the boat, so to speak. But aren't you carrying the roots craze a bit far? I mean — Welsh Week and Arabian Appreciation Afternoon —really!

I : (In a wheezy, breathy voice and with a steely stare that would have gotten me Brando's Oscar as Don Corleone) Have I insulted you? Why do you belittle me, eh *paisano? Mayflower* you say? Let me tell you something: *primo,* the *Mayflower* didn't fly; and *secondo,* at least the Italian ships knew where they were going! Now you know why we don't celebrate Pilgrim Period, *capisco?* Now I suggest you leave before I make you an offer you can't refuse. Have I made my point CONCRETE enough, so to speak, huh?

The Gourmet Gaffe

I have scrimped and scrounged so that I finally saved up the money to treat my wife to a first-class meal at the most posh restaurant in our town — a French affair that has all the trappings for those who want to put on the dog, including a Chief Sneerer (who poses as *Maitre d'*). We arrive for our reservation and as we are being shown to our table we go by a table occupied by the parents of one of my students. I return their "I think I just sat on my salad" smile and as we pass I overhear the husband comment to his wife, "I didn't know *teachers* eat here." After perusing the menu for a while, I excuse myself, go over to their table and fling myself to my knees, screaming and clutching the gentleman's pant legs.

"Good heavens! What have I done? Please, Mr. and Mrs. Schneeze, don't turn me over to the owners. You found me out ... I ... I lied to get in here ... I told them I was a sophisticated lawyer like you. I knew it was wrong but I couldn't help myself. You don't know how hard it is eating in *Bonanza Steakhouses* and *Roy Rogers'*, do you? Oh the nights I've walked by here and have seen swell people eating exquisite cuisine and drinking vintage wines — being served by elegant waiters. I stand outside wishing but knowing the truth . . . that I'm one of THEM, that I'm, Oh God, that I'm just a TEACHER! Please, please just let me have this one moment of bliss, this one chance to feel . . . to feel . . . fulfillment. I promise, no I swear, that I'll never tell another teacher what I saw or did. I swear it! Believe me, I know my place: Those who like to eat at gourmet restaurants do, and those who shouldn't — teach! See, I know my place. Give me this one break . . . please?"

The Obscene Phone Call

We just completed a one-week "art show" in my class featuring my favorite (okay, so it's my only one) work of art, a three-foot high marble copy of Michelangelo's *David,* which I acquired many years ago during a trip to the homeland of my forefathers, Italy. I am just about to open a beer to celebrate *David's* safe return to his pedestal in my living room when the phone rings.

I : Zach Clements here.

Parent: This is Treadwell Trafalgar. I'm calling about . . . about . . . art.

I : Art? Your son's name is Churchill.

Parent: I'm not in the mood for jokes.

I : Sorry.

Parent: Is it true you had a replica of Michelangelo's *David* at you class art show?

I : Yes, a three-foot high marble that's an exact replica. You should have seen it — the kids loved it.

Parent: Perhaps they did, but don't you think that's showing a bit of bad taste, I mean after all, allowing young . . . children to gape at the . . . at the undraped male genitalia. Don't you think it's inappropriate for children in the fourth grade to see that kind of thing.

I : I guess Downs, I mean Churchill — funny about those Freudian slips, once I even called him Winston — didn't tell you about the small fig leaf I hung over *David's,* uhmm, front but it kept falling off him — no, it — no; sorry — I mean . . . you know what I mean! Now concerning the fanny — well, one of the little girls said he, *David* I mean, had nice buns like her brother who's a champion marathoner — so I thought, phooey, I'll let him go barea—, uhmm, that is *bare as* he is. Maybe you're right, though, 'cause a funny thing happened. The first day I had ole Dave at school, the young lady who arrived for class first that morning found his fig leaf lying on the marble base at this feet. "Mr. Clements," she called to me, "where does this leaf thing go on this statue, in its hair or on the piece of wood near the leg?" But, maybe you're right, Square, I mean Battle; sorry, I meant Mr. Trafalgar . . . Darn Freudian, eh?

The Obscene Visitation

The principal, obviously in a state of extreme agitation, arrives at the door of my classroom and requests to speak to me — out in the hall! He tells me Mr. and Mrs. Selfly Rightchus, Perfecta's parents, called very upset over my use of a vulgar word during the class the day before. He tells me that he's invited them to meet with me and him this very afternoon. My initial meeting with the girls field hockey team will have to be cancelled, he says, adding, "This is serious." At 3:10 I enter the office and find the Rightchus' sitting there looking like they just posed for Grant Wood's *American Gothic.*

I : Hello, Mr. and Mrs. Rightchus.

Parent: (Mother) How are you, Mr. Clements. I think you know why we're here: Perfecta came home and said you used the word — I even hate to say it in testimony — the word . . . that also describes a place that holds water . . . during class yesterday. Do you make it a practice to use this kind of street filth in your capacity of builder of our nation's youth?

I : No crap, she did? Did she tell you too that some days I even use four-letter words like sh . . . sh . . . like . . . SHOT!!! Ha! Scared you, didn't I? I'll bet you thought I was going to say the vernacular for, well, you know what for, don't you? Oh, you two devils, I can tell by the red color of your faces you do. Now why are you looking at each other like that? Remember what President Carter told us a few years ago, if you're thinking it you're as guilty as if you said it! I guess the two of you better go wash out your filthy mouths with soap, eh? I recommend *Joy* liquid, because it leaves the tongue squeaky clean and the lips looking younger.

The Touchy-Feely Probe

I was feeling just a little proud, not smug mind you but very content, because here it was the second Friday in May and for the first time this year — for a whole week yet — not one student had called another a meathead, dumb nerd, or the ubiquitous four-letter word and its multiple derivatives. Not even during the usual "Friday final-hour frenzy." Wow! Knock, knock! Someone was at my door . . . .

I : Hello.

Parent: Good afternoon. Are you Mr. Clements?

I : Yes, I am. Won't you come in?

Parent: Yes, thank you. I'm Mrs. Bissonette-Calridder, Cassandra's mother. Yes. Hmm, well to the point then. Dr. Calridder and I were quite, yes, quite dismayed to learn by way of our child's revelations that a boy and girl in your class were actually kissing on the playground. Imagine, second graders kissing! My word! My husband and I were appalled, yes shocked. Do you really think you should permit such brazen behavior?

I : Brazen? Kissing? You should have been here the day we did our classroom production of *Oh Calcutta!* or when we listened to several of Dr. Ruth's tapes on the art of loving. The kids almost got into it those times as much as they did when I started the two new reading groups: The *Penthouse* Pals and the *Gallery* Gang. One bad scene was the day around Thanksgiving when Hal appeared in drag and the girls in the class got real mad. But fundamentally he's a pretty friendly type and no real damage was done. Yep, we're just one intimate happy class. In fact, our motto here is: "The Class That Loves Together Learns Together." Don't you agree, Mrs. Bissonette-Calridder?

The Junk Food Interrogation

I was just sitting down to my lunch in the faculty dining room when a call was put through to me. The caller, who was described by the school telephone receptionist as extremely agitated, had insisted on being put through to me despite the fact it was my lunch time.

I : (Long pause)

Parent: Mr. Clements? Are you there?

I : Is that an existential question?

Parent: Mr. Clements, this is Elizabeth Hadley, Chuck's mother. I'm very concerned about what's going on in the cafeteria.

I : What's that?

Parent: Chuck tells me he trades his celery and carrot sticks for potato chips and his apple for *Twinkies.*

I : Hmmm. I knew there was some kind of dealing going on.

Parent: It's got to stop. I don't want Chuck to grow up to be a wild-eyed junk food sugar maniac. I hope you can assist on this problem.

I : (The sound of rattling is heard.)

Parent: I'm sorry Mr. Clements. What did you say?

I : I'm sorry. I wanted to make a note about our conversation and I was looking for my pen. Thought I dropped it in the bag of potato chips. No, maybe it's under the bag of *Oreos.* Whoops, just spilled my *Coke* on my *Milky Way.* Mrs. Hadley, can I get back to you after my dinner?

"People say you call me a "vocal new board member." What I'd love to know is what you really think of me, T.C."

8

ON BEING TAKEN BY A GRADUATE COURSE

Of all the unflattering, mostly unfair descriptions of teachers, the allegation we are gluttons for punishment is probably the most well deserved. How else can you explain why teachers would take a grad course during the teaching year? Granted, sometimes due to extenuating circumstances the years slip by and a teacher lacking a permanent certificate suddenly realizes he or she must complete three or six hours of grad work in order to remain employed the following September. But these instances in no way account for the number of classroom weary teachers who every fall and spring semester trudge off to some university at the end of a tough day of teaching. Money? It is true that for every four to six hours of additional grad credit earned, a teacher receives a salary increment, and as everyone knows, additional dollars are always an important issue.

But in this case, these dollars can only be described as *blood* money. Too harsh? Perhaps you think me too hard on educators? Consider what happened to me and a colleague last winter and then tell me who took what from whom.

"It's cancelled, right Mandy?" I called to my passing colleague who teaches English to freshmen at our high school. I was inquiring about whether the university had called off the evening's slate of grad classes due to the snow storm that was raging outside.

"No," she replied. "Can you believe that?" The tone of her voice reflected exactly my own keen sense of incredulity. "Know where we can rent a dogsled?" she called to me as she turned to head up the stairs.

At 2:30 that afternoon her joke about a dogsled didn't seem so funny. Cars were off the road every which way. Visibility was almost zero and the snow was now falling at blizzard proportions as everyone except the university officials knew it was going to. "If it were any professor other than Hardbutt, I'd suggest we bag it Mandy, but you know her policy about cuts," I said as we crept along the highway between our school and the U some six miles distant.

"Tell me about it," replied my passenger. "If I didn't have to pass this course to keep my job next year, I assure you I would skip no matter what. But I don't understand why you worry about the grade or, for that matter, why you are even taking the course when you don't have to. What did you say you have, 35 hours beyond the Masters? You've got a permanent certificate. Why the heck do you put yourself through this?"

"Money," I answered. "This will put me on the Masters plus 40 step next year. And you know we're looking at our kid's college tuition in a few years."

"I hope he doesn't get to use your life insurance proceeds for college," Mandy replied as we passed an accident that had not one ambulance on the scene, but two. How we did it I'm not sure but at 3:55 P.M. we pulled into the university parking area where buried cars made it now resemble a drumlin farm. "Grab my scarf," I called to Mandy as I leaned into the maelstrom and headed for what I believed was the direction of Hamilton Hall, the building where our class was held. I wanted her to hold on to my scarf so that we would not become separated. Present conditions almost guaranteed such a separation would lead to one or both of us becoming a drumlin of our own. After what seemed an interminable trek we stumbled into Hamilton.

A quick stop at the coffee machine and we hurried to our class. Wonder of wonders, our notoriously punctilious prof was actually a minute late. As she called the class to order, I looked about and noticed that all the teacher-students in attendance were, like Mandy and me, individuals who had already taken their one allowed cut. You see our prof (recall the epithet Hardbutt) allowed one cut after which your grade went down one letter per absence regardless of the reason. I knew her nickname was well deserved when I requested that our cuts, Mandy and mine, not count against us since we were attending an assembly honoring the President of the United States who was visiting our school to bestow a School of Excellence award upon our faculty and student body. Hardbutt replied, "If you choose to use your one cut frivolously, that's your affair. But be aware that on your next absence a letter grade penalty will be assessed."

"It's 4:05. May we begin," intoned Hardbutt, actually Professor Evelyn Biggs-Larimer, BA, MS, Ph.D., the last from Harvard no less. "Our topic for today is motivation. Motivation was first seen in the Greek culture. The word derives from the Greek mote to move...."

Ah, another journey into the esoteric, I thought to myself. *What's the old adage about practicing what one preaches? Motivation? My students would eat up this phony. She wouldn't last five minutes in a real classroom.* With those thoughts, my mind began to wander. I assumed my "pretend you're interested" look. Over the many grad courses I had taken, I learned how to affect that look to perfection. It was time for my favorite sport. I got the biggest charge out of watching other students slowly begin to fade. The eyelids become heavy until the eyes are but narrow slits. Then the chin drops to the chest, at which point the head immediately snaps back up, the eyes opening but a bit more. Then the process repeats. The other fade-move I loved to watch was one I termed the "head swivel maneuver." That's when a student dozes and as they nod off their head swivels back from one side to the other; at the end of said swivel the dozer usually wakens with an embarrassed start. I love catching their eye at that point and snickering at them. It is cruel, but fun. And besides, it was how I stayed awake. And today, no doubt as a result of the hazardous drive in, the faders were in particularly good form. Madam Professor was just beginning to discuss motivation development in the Dark Ages, when I too was seized by acute fatigue exacerbated by the temperature in the room, which I'm sure was in excess of ninety. But I knew how to handle this. Time to get clever. I rested my left elbow on the desk and used my left hand as a prop for my head, my fingers becoming an eye shade to prevent the instructor from seeing my eyes closing for brief periods. The open notebook and my right hand clutching a pen poised to record all the pearls of wisdom being offered, completed this clever ruse. Clearly you can tell I was a past master at this game of undetected academic slumber. I drifted....

Horrors! I awoke to find myself drooling, a continuous bead of saliva extending from the left corner of my mouth to a large wet spot just above my breast pocket. My previously fail-safe pen hand had traced a seismographic line which railed off the notebook page and onto the desk surface. The markings resembled the pattern of an eight on the Richter Scale. As I cast my eyes upward toward the instructor, I found her staring directly at me. I immediately went into a stretch while affecting a nonchalant "I wasn't sleeping you know" look which I instantly realized she wasn't buying; after all, the spit thing was in full view. I did the only thing I could do . . . look away. A legend had proved mortal. Were I a Japanese student, hara- kiri would have been performed . . . immediately! Sheer face loss prevented any further soporific exercises, but the damage had been done. I spent the remaining hour of the class deciding on a plan to rescue some status. I, a veteran course taker, had to eat crow. And Hardbutt hated coaches like me anyway.

When the class ended at 7:00, I immediately rushed up to my unmasker and requested her suggestions for outside readings to further supplement the stimulating lecture just delivered. She knew I was lying, I knew I was lying, but the academic game must be played by the rules. When all else fails, pretend. Use flattery. Over the semester I had tried to impress this important survival skill on dear Mandy, but she refused to be mollified, citing the importance of her time and how she resented having to take courses that were basically a waste of her energies. Each drive home after our class she would rail at the hours we had just wasted. The time she almost lost it completely, however, was following the last class meeting of this course, when we handed in our fifteen-page plus term papers. On the way down the stairs, Mandy said, "Can you imagine we pay money for this crap? I've had it. I don't care what happens, I'm going right back up there and tell that woman exactly what a horse's pitute I think she is."

"Whoa," I said. "Let's discuss this over a beer." Fortunately, she agreed but I could tell she was still fuming. An hour or so later, after our third *Miller*, she began to listen to reason. I think what finally got to her was when I asked if she had plans to enter another field since she would have no job should she fail this course as surely she would were she to take action. Her reply: "I'll wait until we get our grades, then I'll go tell Hardbutt exactly what I think."

"Good, now you're using good sense," I replied with relief, for I was certain my grade would also be affected because we did come to class together and the prof knew we taught in the same school. "I'll go in with you," I cried with great bravado. "Now let's have one more to celebrate our having made it through with only the one cut."

Later that evening, on our way home, reality set in. Though neither of us verbalized it, we both realized we weren't going in to blast Hardbutt or any of the other impostors at the U. Why? No doubt it was the realization that we could blast all we want, nothing would change because of a long-recognized truism of education (with notable exceptions of course): *"Those who can, teach, and those who can't, teach teachers."*

9

THE CLASSROOM AS THEATER

I stared at the document detailing the major charges upon which the School Board was considering dismissing me from my tenured faculty position.

CHARGE NUMBER ONE: Leaving a classroom filled with students unattended.

CHARGE NUMBER TWO: Burdening the School Board with a lawsuit brought by the SPCA charging cruelty to animals.

CHARGE NUMBER THREE: Causing the School Board to answer fire code violation charges brought by the City Fire Marshall.

CHARGE NUMBER FOUR: Inciting a near riot caused by deliberate setting of a fire in a social studies classroom.

I'm innocent. Now understand, I do not deny the specific items the board charges happened, but I feel they are taken out of context. In fact, considering my teaching philosophy is centered around using "ham," theatricality, if you will, in the teaching of my students, I believe I have a strong case for a counter suit alleging I'm being harassed and denied academic freedom. Let me first, however, respond to each specific charge.

Charge number one, leaving a classroom full of students unattended, resulted from my attempts to register, dramatically, my concern over my seventh grade biology class' performance on a unit test. I believed them totally prepared for this test only to find their scores indicated no one had prepared for it. After returning the test papers I said not a word, just stared at the students. The uncharacteristic silence was deafening. The discomfort level rose. Several students coughed. Others exchanged anxious glances while others shuffled their feet or squirmed in their seats. When the silence reached a crescendo, I turned my back to the class, mimicking Olivier in a courtroom scene from one of his classic movies and stared off at the distant snow covered hills. The panoramic view added to the illusion that this third-floor classroom was much, much higher than that. I, at last, broke the silence.

"Is this performance indicative of what you think of me and what we have been learning?" I asked. "Then I have no need to go on living." With that I threw open the window and flung myself over the sill. Hearing the students' screams of terror while I hurtled through space brought me deep feelings of satisfaction, feelings which definitely helped, moments later, lessen the numbing pain. I'm a ham but I'm not crazy.

This stunt wasn't done without preparation, without rehearsal. No way. However, the day before when I had rehearsed it, I had jumped out the second window from the front and it went smooth as silk, the huge snow banks making the whole thing nothing for a guy in as good shape as I. But today, during the actual "performance" I went out the first window. Arrrrgh! The snow bank under this window, if anything, was even deeper than the one under the first window I had used. It wasn't the snow bank, the problem was my memory. I forgot about the bicycle rack buried under the snow in this area.

The pain of straddling a steel bicycle rack after a slightly cushioned jump from three stories up can only be described as paralyzing. But I didn't scream. Let the record show I threw up, but I didn't scream. Why? The students would then have had the last laugh. No way I could let that happen. Indeed, it was their screams I continued to enjoy as I crawled toward the B entrance, determined none of them would see me thus physically humbled. I could feel the clamminess of my sweat-soaked shirt as I slowly got to my feet, just to my feet, happy I didn't faint even though I was safely out of any student's line of vision. You've heard the expression "the show must go on," well that's what I realized I had to do. Guts it out. I knew my face was cadaverous pale and the swelling in my crotch made walking agonizing beyond description, but I willed myself to walk back into the classroom. What a triumph!

"Scared you, didn't I?" I asked the kids, many of whom were unabashedly crying. "I could have been killed as a result of your poor performance," I continued in my hoarse, Godfather voice, not at all faked, I might add. "I hope you will never again let this happen." As you might suspect, this episode has gained folklore status with many hundred times the thirty students who were present claiming to have witnessed the event. I still hear students twenty-five years later when I return exam papers whisper, "I hope he doesn't take a Brodie out the window again." The fact I now teach on the ground floor doesn't seem to affect their recollection of the famous suicide attempt. Legends, after all, have a life of their own, right?

Sometimes, I'm sure my gimmicks for a lesson are what a few people would regard as in poor taste. Perhaps that's what got the SPCA hot and bothered, you know charge number two. All I wanted to do was demonstrate, unforgettably, characteristics of living and dead organisms. I decided to do my Frankenstein Doctor number and bring in a dead dog, which had been struck by a car. You should have heard the screams when I whipped off the white sheet covering the dog and shouted, "Vee vill bring heem bakk to life." Or, speaking of questionable taste, the time I had the kids listen to a recording that went: "Thump, thuh, thump, thuh, thump." That's all, just those sounds repeated over and over. "What is it?" I questioned the now thoroughly puzzled learners. When none but the one smarty who guessed everything had a clue, I shouted, "This is what it is," and at that pulled from a bag and held aloft a huge, bloody cow heart that continued to drip blood even as I held it above the desk of one of the sweetest young ladies in the class.

As usual when I do this lesson, the screams of "gross" and "disgusting" were again shouted. The two or three students close to barfing or actually doing so, including the sweet young thing in the front row, were also quite normal. Odors aside, I rate such reactions as five stars; boffo; a smash. Okay, so the dowdy SPCA spoils things unnecessarily. But, what a learning environment, eh?

Charges three and four are really related and both are without merit when you realize I was just trying to stimulate student interest. The idea for the lesson sounded so perfect, a sure fire winner: The Zeppelin Hindenburg Disaster . . . Live! Admit it, doesn't that stroke your imagination just hearing the title? Though I planned to use the idea in my social studies class, the concept certainly captivated my colleagues in the science department, particularly the chairman. Boy, their interest really fooled me, but then again how could I have known this enthusiasm masked an assassination plot masterminded by the chairman? Whose assassination? Mine, of course. My purpose in using the Hindenburg was to bring the students a vivid example of Hitler and the Nazis' preoccupation with propaganda. This was, of course, related to the events leading up to the outbreak of the Second World War. I needed a gimmick to give the lesson, uhhm, here's that word again, pizzazz.

"Why not fill a plastic dry cleaning bag with natural gas after its edges are sealed to form a balloon-like vehicle and put a match to it to stimulate the Hindenburg's destruction," proposed the Brutus yet unknown to me.

"A good idea but too dangerous. It might explode, right?" I replied.

"Nah, it's like lighter fluid; poof, and the flame would be over. No sweat, but plenty dramatic," he reassured me, that white frocked snake in the grass.

"All right then," I fairly shouted. "That's the kind of stuff I love." He really had hit my hot button on this one. Later, as I ruefully reflected on that fateful conversation, I realized I should have done a test run just like I did with most of my way-out ideas. But why should I have doubted Stanley? How was I to know it was his brother-in-law's dog I tried to bring back to life? Anyway, here is what transpired.

The introduction to the lesson was great. I used Edward R. Murrow's *You Are There* recording which featured the live report of a reporter-eye witness account about the tragedy at Lakehurst, New Jersey in 1934. I used the length of the B wing as a model to enable the students to appreciate the immense size of the airship. You may recall, as the reporter gives his matter-of-fact report on the docking of the gigantic zeppelin, he suddenly screams that the airship is on fire and begins his now immortal observations detailing the destruction of the craft and the death of many of its passengers. The students leaned in, obviously entranced by what they were hearing.

"Want to see what happened?" I asked, knowing full well what their response would be.

"Yeah," they shouted in one voice.

I stepped over to the huge clear plastic balloon with the large black swastika on the crude tail and put a match to it. W H H H O O O O O O O O O S S S H H H H H! the ball of flame instantly claimed my eyebrows, tie, sideburns, and . . . courage. I remember screaming, "Run away!" as I went to the floor. The rest of the episode is a blur. The principal was in the room in seconds and the city fire department in minutes. Fortunately, only a few students suffered very minor scrapes in the panic that followed the fire and only minor damage occurred to the classroom ceiling.

I guess this particular lesson was what ultimately caused the Board to take action and bring charges against me. The worst part of the ordeal is sweating out this week, waiting to appear before the Board to face possible dismissal and perhaps even criminal charges, or so the rumor mill has it. The other tough part of the affair is having to endure the wise comments like the one concerning my looks: "When are you auditioning for Mr. Spock's understudy," or the student who commented, "Mr. C, you were really scared weren't you? I never saw anyone crawl as fast as you did."

I can defend myself even though rumor has it at least one teacher, Mortimer Greenhouse, was testifying against me at the hearing. "Bizarre behavior, eh?" Is that how Ole' Greenhouse plans to describe my teaching style? That remark from a person who regards Mona Lisa's look as inappropriately comical, causes me no offense. I'm not even surprised to be honest. Anyway, I can't give his comment a whole lot of credence because he never forgave me for what I once said to him about his perpetual frown. I guess he *really* didn't like me asking if he was practicing to be a popsicle because he looked like he had a broom stuck in him. Oh well.

Now don't get me wrong. On a scale from one to ten, one being a teacher whose level of animation caused the principal on several occasions to hold a mirror in front of this person's mouth to determine whether the rescue squad should be summoned and ten being a teacher whose students find it necessary to take massive doses of tranquilizers with their cookies and milk, I'm a ten, plus, plus. Bragging? Hyperbole? Neither, but you be the judge. I'm not a showoff, so don't try dismissing me as some screwball exhibitionist. Let me hasten to point out, as I did to the Board, that my use of ham is solidly backed by educational research. I trust you are familiar with Clements' work on effective teaching which cites the three H's: Head, Heart and Ham. As the noted researcher writes, the effective teacher must possess all three; I confess to having more of the last H than the other two, both of which I also possess I might add.

Why do I place such emphasis on being a ham when teaching? Consider the students we teach today. These kids are weaned on giant screen television, quad sound, trips into outer space, and total immersion in the world of *vivid, lifelike* experiences. It is, therefore, my opinion a lesson that does not fairly come alive is doomed to failure.

Consider this actual experience. During a unit on World War II, a colleague of mine, a Colonel in the Reserves, in an attempt to get realism in his unit, pulled strings and requisitioned an eighty-ton Patton tank from the local armory. He drove the tank the four miles from the National Guard Center and pulled it up onto the high school lawn and parked it outside his classroom. Students were blown away, right? Wrong. Instead of "Oh wow," what he got was "Gimme a break." In fact, the only thing that saved him from a total loss of face was the burst watermain caused by the immense weight of the tank. Apparently, the fact that two scuba divers had to be summoned to salvage the school's collection of trophies did net the Colonel some positive press from the students. Doubtless, had he been able to take out a tree or two or flatten a car Rambo style, the kids would have voted him teacher of the year on the spot. Get what I'm saying. Today, pizzazz is the name of the game.

That's exactly why I teach as I do. It's risky, but dedicated pedagogues as far back as Socrates have known that not everybody is proffering a toast to your skills when they hand you a goblet. I could go on, but by now you have the picture. Now I'm not going to kid you and pretend that this kind of teaching is without risk, I mean you already know how Greenhouse feels. Oh no, you run the risk of getting a lot more people upset than just one odd ball.

Man, I've been called in on the carpet so many times that the seat of my pants are worn out. As mentioned, the dead dog lesson, high voltage jolts and all, did not bring the dog back to life but sure got the SPCA's attention . . . and the superintendent's. The heart lesson also never fails to get me in trouble with the custodians. It seems they take umbrage over having to clean up the semi-digested breakfast of the fainthearted witnesses to learning drama . . . every year! But you learn to live with the risks. I guess, at the core, a ham loves to court disaster; it adds excitement to the process of performing. Think about it, wondering each time you go out of the blocks: will I get fired for this one? But risky or not, a true ham constantly reaches for ever greater realism.

All this said, I'm not really worried, you know, *really* worried. Hey, a dedicated ham has to pay a price for his art and if a pinkslip is that price, then so be it. But if it comes to that, I'll make them feel so guilty, they won't have a moment's peace for the rest of their lives.

My plan? I'm going to add another H to Head, Heart and Ham; H for hanging as with a noose. Talk about a class move, listen to this and tell me it isn't a master plot. I can see it all now, thousands of students in tears at the funeral service, Board members recalled by angry citizens, school administrators driven from office by marauding mobs. What a delicious idea. I can hardly contain myself. In fact, know what? It's crazy, but the more I think about his great ending, the more I worry they *won't* fire me and I will not get to do this great bit.

Hold it, how can I even for a minute think that might happen? You see, I've even got the whole final scene played out in my head. Not at home, no people; the flagpole would be technically impossible; the cafeteria would be in poor taste. But get this, the crossbar of the goal posts in our endzone during the halftime ceremonies of the Homecoming Game, on the third of November, right after they play the alma mater, Roar Lions Roar.

Brilliant, right?

Are we talking ham genius here or what?

"There she is, right on time!"

10

HAVE LESSON...WILL TRAVEL

W ebster's New Collegiate Dictionary defines tutor as "a person charged with the instruction and guidance of another; a private teacher." The word, in my opinion, is the ultimate oxymoron. I define it as "one who loses his self-esteem, often; who falls victim to the almighty buck and can easily go to the dogs, literally." How do I know this? I'm one of the few who took his briefcase on the road and lived to tell the tale.

How could something as innocent as the desire to supplement one's income have degenerated into the dark comedy it became? Looking back, it appears the warning signs were all there, but once blinded by the possibility of augmented income, all else yielded to accommodation. I considered clerking? Too boring. Waitering? Too long hours. Sales? Too unpredictable. What could I do that would allow me to use my pedagogical skills, tailor hours to my wishes and bring in as much income as, say a sanitation worker in most cities? The answer came while I was attending the National Middle Schools Conference. I happened to mention my dilemma to a hotshot attendee from Scarsdale, New York. "Money? Teaching skill? Own schedule? You want to make ten to fifteen K, no sweat? If you got the teaching gift, that is, all you've got to do is take your act *on the road*. In no time you will be planning Easter in Barbados and calling the decorator to get the old home place looking like something." So counselled the man in the silk suit and Italian slippers. I should argue?

On the plane flying home, my plan took shape. It all seemed so simple. I certainly was regarded as one of the most gifted teachers on the faculty and very popular with students. Overhead would be negligible, and you could charge more per hour because Johnny or Jill wouldn't have to be transported. And you could choose when to work and when not to work. Perfect. Too good to be true. I forgot one thing: Remember the old adage, "If something sounds too good to be true, it probably is."

After the announcement of my availability became public, I was inundated with requests for my service and too busy multiplying hours by dollars to worry about old adages. Plus, my wife and I were occupied looking at carpeting samples and travel brochures. I selected five of the parents waving checkbooks at me and put the other dozen on hold. I remember thinking to myself as I arrived at the home of my initial client contact, *man, you are dynamite. You better start subscribing to the Wall Street Journal.* How could I have known that in short order the only subscription I would be seeking was the *Journal of Abnormal Psychology*?

The meet and greet were cordial. Momma says that Cyrus is low in comprehension and vocabulary. Cy and I adjourn to his room, er, suite, to begin remaking his scholastic persona. I administered the heavy-duty diagnostic battery and discover Cyrus is weak in comprehension and vocabulary. Time to test attitudes.

I: So what do you think is preventing you from doing better on this stuff, Cyrus?

C: Reading stinks.

I: (I ignore. Time to get high energy motivational on him.) "Don't kid me, Cy. Everyone wants to do better, right?"

C: How long do you stay?

I: How are you going to get through high school?

C: We done yet?

I: (Time to call his bluff.) Maybe you would rather I not come to help you?

C: Right.

I: (This was getting serious. My teaching pride was getting hammered and my twenty for next week was rapidly fading. Time to do the psychological flip.) "Well, that answer just tells me you really do want me to help. Everyone wants to do better in something as important as reading, you have to admit that?

C: Reading stinks.

I: (Without consulting my watch, I decided that today's lesson was over so I went into my strong close.) "Well, it is time to stop for today. Why don't you take some time this week to think about what we discussed. See if you can't come up with a more positive outlook, okay?"

C: Reading stinks.

As I, alone, descended the curving polished mahogany staircase to the Italian marble entryway resembling a swollen checkerboard, I had hoped to slip out and be spared the agony of reporting the futility of my initial efforts, but luck was against me. Momma stood on a black square and I on a white; she appeared as an imposing queen, me a humble pawn.

M: So it is kind of hopeless, isn't it?

I: Hopeless? Madam, I already see positive signs.

C: Reading stinks. (Cy's voice rains down from the landing above.)

M: For that remark young man you are confined to your room until dinner.

I: (*I think to myself: Confined? Punishment? Giant T.V., stocked frig, Palomar class telescope, stereo, private bath, and walls covered with the Playboy centerfolds from the last decade's issues.*) Could you book me in for a week? (I utter sotto voce.)

M: Pardon me?

I: Good, you brook no such speech.

M: Would you like payment now?

I: No thank you. Why don't I bill you at the end of each month.

(Does this woman regard me a common fishmonger or tradesman? How could she think for a minute I would allow filthy lucre to sully a professional call?) Don't fret dear lady. Cyrus is in good hands.

I almost tripped going out the door because I had my fingers, eyes and legs crossed at that last statement. But at least I was still on the payroll. Driving home, I searched for some small positive observation concerning the dismal initial effort with Cyrus. It wasn't easy, but by the time I pulled into my driveway forty minutes later, I had discovered something to smile about after all, *at least he didn't say I stink.*

Little did I realize that this was only the beginning of the daily assaults on what was once the most solidly built professional self-image on the faculty. But that image was based on the task of meeting the needs of children who were in need and in the main, appreciated your sincere attempts to meet those needs. In private tutoring, however, the ground rules are all different. When the idea for hiring a tutor originates, is enforced and perpetuated by the parents *without* the support and enthusiastic participation of the tutee, the person in greatest need usually turns out to be the tutor! In the vast majority of instances, it's not that the Cyruses of the world can't learn but that they don't want to learn. They conjure up the most creative ways imaginable to make that point clear to one and all, but especially to the hired briefcase.

In addition to the student authored putdowns, the lifestyles of the wealthy — and that was the status of 99% of those who could afford twenty to thirty dollars an hour — represented an even greater threat to one's self-esteem. Consider my arrival at the second home I *deigned* to honor with *my* presence.

The circular driveway took three minutes to navigate from one entrance to the massive entryway of the huge Tudor styled mansion. Upon pressing the doorbell, I was greeted not with the pedestrian ding-dong sounds of chimes, but with the theme of "Rule Britannia." No human voice responded; rather from within I heard the bark of what was obviously a very large dog, barking that was initially muted but grew progressively louder as though the beast approached from a very great distance. WHAM! The massive steel-banded oak door actually appeared to buckle as the cur hurled itself against it. A childhood dog attack left me with an uncontrollable fear of the canine species, a fear now rekindled to panic proportions by the obvious antisocial behaviors of the animal within. I lurched backward, flight a distinct consideration as it appeared ever more likely the door was about to become a drawbridge. Suddenly, a voice called from a leaded window in the turret above.

"Dr. Clements, is that you?"

"If this be the manor of the Browns, then in sooth it is I." (Tudor houses make me feel Shakespearean in speech.)

"Oh splendid. Sorry about Tito's greeting. He's really a very nice dog. He loves to put on his vicious watchdog routine for visitors."

"Well, I must admit he certainly has caused me to cancel any consideration of burglarizing the premises. I hope you don't need to employ a carpenter to repair the door that I suspect is about to be unhinged," I responded.

"This may sound crazy but I wonder if you might help me calm Tito. Now don't laugh. I'm going to go to the door at the kitchen wing to your right and open, then quickly shut the door. Tito will think you are coming in that door and will rush to that entrance. When he does, you come into the front door, which is unlocked, and go up the stairs. Ashley will be waiting for you at the top of the landing. I know this is odd, but don't laugh."

Laugh? By this time I was about to go to my knees, convulsing. The only thing that saved me was the fact that I had stuffed a hanky in my mouth, thus preventing peals of laughter from drowning out the voice imploring sobriety. With no small amount of trepidation, I advanced upon the door, my scent foiling any attempt at stealth as the dog's renewed frenzy attested.

"Oh, look who is here," a distant voice called out followed by a slam of a door off to the right. From within, the sounds of rapidly receding din confirmed that dog had, indeed, fallen for Madam's ruse. I quickly entered, prepared despite the outlined ploy, to hastily retreat should any sign of the dog become manifest.

"Dr. Clements. Up here. Hurry!" a voice called to me from above.

I spied Ashley, an eighth-grader at my school, standing on the balcony several stories up. Her use of the term "hurry" added urgency to my movement and I literally took three to four steps per stride.

"Woof. Snarl. Bark. Gnnnash." Tito, obviously not this man's best friend, appeared from out of nowhere and began to take the stairs . . . five at a time.

Heart pounding, face flushed, I gained the landing and started running after Ashley who was half way down a spacious corridor. A coronary was clearly imminent, yet my leaden legs somehow manage to propel me toward the open door at which Ashley had stationed herself.

"Hurry," she screamed just short of hysterically. "He's gaining!"

That comment's effect on my adrenaline reserve was sufficient to enable me to launch a dive which carried me through the doorway. I landed belly first upon the carpet which thankfully was thickly padded. Wham! Ashley whipped the door closed as my feet cleared the opening, then put her full weight against it. Slam! Tito hit the door. Bam! Ashley hit the floor. Mercifully, the door did not cave in.

"You okay?" Ashley inquired from her prone position next

to me. I didn't answer. I was preoccupied with recalling the symptoms of the onset of cardiac arrest. "Dr. Clements, are you all right?" My co-recliner once more inquired, her voice now tinged with genuine concern.

"I think so," I finally responded, somewhat surprised the fabled hot anvil had not fallen on my chest . . . yet! "But I'm afraid it will be necessary to have our lesson lying down. I don't think I have the strength to make it to a sitting position, at least not immediately."

Why lie? The lesson was a washout. I was too concerned about my departure scenario to give Ashley my full attention, who, by the way, turned out not to have any scholastic needs for me to remediate but merely wanted me for a tutor because her best friend Sherry was on my list of tutees. Once respiring normally, I reconnoitered the windows in hopes of finding a fire escape, or at least a sturdy trellis. No luck. Finally, I flat out asked Ashley. "How does one get out of your house, eh? Tell me that before you finish responding to the vocabulary test, please."

"That's no problem. Mother will again pretend someone is at the side door and while Tito is out there, I'll show you out the front."

Show? The kid's got a way with words, I think to myself. *Show as in run for my life . . . !* "Why doesn't your mom just put the dog in the basement or shut it up in another room?" I then asked.

"He has already scratched his way completely through two doors and has severely damaged three others. Now don't get me wrong. He just continues to act like a puppy, you know, frisky and all."

"Frisky equals five doors destroyed? Well, if you say so. So until next week, Ashley. I guess I'm ready to run the gauntlet," I answered. My apprehension was increasing as I recalled the look on her face when she yelled, 'Hurry, he's gaining.' "Whoops, where's my hat?"

While I searched the room for my fedora, Ashley buzzed her mother on the intercom to coordinate my departure. No hat was to be found. I said, "I must have left it in the car, Ashley, but if you find it, keep it for me until next week, okay?"

"Ready?" she asked while cracking the door slightly and listening intently. "Now!" she fairly hissed and with that we both rushed out the door. I quickly gained the lead which I increased by eight paces as I started down the stairs; the dash was made much easier with the aid of gravity. "My fedora," I wheezed between four tread leaps while gesturing to the gray felt shreds littering the scarlet stair carpeting. "Oh, that naughty Tito," hissed Ashley now many steps behind me.

Snarls drawing louder by the second drown out her voice. "Darn. Here he comes," I screamed. I knew I had eight more steps and a twelve-foot foyer to cover. How far did Tito have to come?

"Tito. Tito. Come here you bad dog," Mrs. was screaming loudly in the distance.

"Tito. Tito, you bad dog," Ashley was screaming even more loudly.

"Tito. Tito, I'm not a door!" I screamed loudest of all.

With a final Herculean leap I went from the fourth step half way across the foyer. One final thrust and I was out the door which I slammed violently. Thuddd! Once more Tito went into his door destroyer routine, clearly intent on adding the oak to his already impressive tally. The euphoria of escape overwhelmed me. The need for strong drink and the tranquility of home beckoned me. I strode resolutely toward my car. "ARRRRG.G...G.HHH!" I gasped as a violent jerk at my neck stopped my breathing, walking, and . . . standing. The next thing I knew I was seated in slush, the icy, wet cold inundating pants, undershorts and everything else! Presently, I realized with some relief that I had not been the victim of a suburban mugging but that my extra long Harvard scarf caught in the door during flight had become a crimson leash now tethering me door to neck.

"You all right, Dr. Clements?" the unseen voice from the second floor once more intoned.

Answers like "kiss my butt" and "you'll hear from my lawyer" raced through my mind, but I remembered that I was there of my own volition and therefore responded, "Fine. Just slipped on the ice."

"Oh sorry. Have a nice day."

All the way home I seethed over having to do a Mack Sennett routine. *I'm a tutor, not a comedian,* I thought to myself. *I need this?* Well, I worked with, visited with anyway, Ashley for three years, so the answer is rather obvious. It took some adjustments, to be sure, because the Tito routine minus the garotting and hat dismantling, of course, were standard procedure. I learned to dress in light clothes sans fedora, to wear sneakers and to do calisthenics followed by warm-up wind sprints prior to ringing the doorbell. How did I rationalize such face loss? I reasoned the physical workout at the Browns enabled me to skip my workout at the health club, thus permitting me to get home earlier on Friday evenings. In effect, I was getting paid for a workout. How could any reasonably sane person walk away from that?

The Tito encounters were but the beginning of my canine capers that ultimately led to my decision to give up life on the road. It became clear that most households in need of a tutor had an even more urgent need for a dog obedience trainer. If only I had dual certification in Reading and Dog Obedience, I could have cleaned up. Instead, I got run off. Oddly enough, it wasn't the Tito type dogs that did me in but the overly affectionate kind . . . like Pierre.

"This is Pierre," cooed Sally that first day I visited her home. I almost laughed at the large French poodle-type dog's appearance: spats above the feet, topiary-type tail and collar, and that pompadour on the head gave him a Little Richard-like appearance. I leaned over to give the required petting but instead had to use both hands to protect myself as Pierre thrust his snout into my crotch and nuzzled deeply. "Whhoooa," I exclaimed, trying unsuccessfully to escape.

"Don't be alarmed, Dr. Clements. He's just...." "I know," I interrupted, "trying to tell me he likes me. Being friendly, right?" Too late. He had already slobbered all over my freshly pressed khakis.

"Pierre, you naughty boy. You have got the man's pants all wet. I'll get you a cloth with cold water on it."

"No, it's okay, Sal. Let's get started. Where do we work?"

"If you say so. We are going to work down the hall in the study. Just follow me. Pierre, you stay!"

As we made our way down the hall, I inquired bout the wood panelling. "Is this cherry or pi . . . Whooooiiiy!!" I exclaimed as I literally leaped onto Sally's back driving her to the floor.

"What the . . ." she screamed, trying to crawl out from under me. Upon seeing my face; however, her vexation turned to laughter. She roared 'til she was near tears.

"It was Pierre's fault," I stammered. "He came up behind me and, and, well...."

"He snuffed you. He snuffs people he really likes," Sally explained while she wiped the tears from her cheeks.

"Snuffed. Is that what you call it when he sticks his nose up er, up, well, you know, up! Is he in heat or something?"

Pierre, for his part, stood looking innocently down at the two of us lying in the hall having this bizarre conversation. He was smiling. Don't tell me he didn't know exactly what he was doing. And so it went. Every visit to Sally's was a test of my ability to know Pierre's exact location in relation to my person. Sal's parents got used to my suddenly whirling about — in mid-conversation — to affect an anti-snuff posture. Likewise, they got used to seeing me suddenly vault the coffee table because Pierre caught me off guard.

What really drove me crazy was the way the masters of

these creatures would justify the behavior of their pets. The most obnoxious activities would be defined as "he's just showing you he likes you" or "he's being friendly." What makes these people think a guest finds it pleasant to be sitting in a low slung settee enjoying a cup of tea and having a large Irish Setter place his huge snout inches from your face and into it, waft hot, moist breaths reeking of liver, horse, ash and God knows what all? Likes me? Say what? Foul is what it is!

I should have known that it would only be a matter of time before I would begin to develop genuine hostility toward ill-behaved dogs, hostility that began to affect my performance as a teacher. I used to fantasize about snuffing one of these "pets" . . . with my pointy wingtips. The day fantasy became reality was the day I quit the road.

I was tutoring two sisters who had the most obnoxious — there's that word again — pugnosed yipper that carried on from the moment I arrived until I left. I could have stood the constant yipping, but the little rat, despite what his masters considered stern commands to "stay down," continually would jump onto my leg and claw frantically at my trousers. He completely redesigned two separate pairs of double knits — I had them made into knickers — but under no circumstances was I going to wear puttees or spats for tutoring. No scolding would make Dukey, that was his name, desist. Finally, one day while the lady of the house was fetching my coat, he started the clawing routine again. "Down," I shouted, "Down!" Then, I decided, was the time. "Dukey, get it," I shouted, pretending to throw something toward the opposite wall. When he turned to catch the flight of the invisible object, I let him have it! What a glorious feeling to watch the gray ball of fur fly across the room and splat against the far wall.

His yipping brought Madam on the run. "What happened to my little Dukey?" she cooed over and over. "I think he caught his tail on the chair leg," I responded, my face a picture of choirboy innocence as I gestured to him licking his hind under the blue Queen Anne chair where he had taken refuge.

Two weeks after launching Dukey, I was off the road, poorer, but emotionally in much better shape than I had been in years. I miss the income every once in a while, but then I see the Young Turk, to whom I turned over all my clients, preparing to head out at the close of a school day. As I watch him get into his track suit and sneakers and start loading his pockets and briefcase with dog biscuits, all monetary concerns vanish. Plus, if I ever do get into financial trouble and experience harassment by bill collectors, I'll get Tito or Dukey and turn 'em loose. "Hey, he's just being friendly," I'll shout as the collectors run off the property.

11

COACHES' DISEASE

No, Coach, my best friend for over twenty-five years, has not always acted as he does now. Hardly! When he first joined our faculty he came across as quiet, easy going, soft-spoken, the archetypical Vermont Yankee. Surprised? No doubt, especially if you saw him on the sidelines during a Friday night ball game you would have every reason to find that description hard to believe. So would I. Continually pacing, chin rubbing, crotch tugging, belt adjusting, shoulder shrugging, ear pulling, neck rubbing, arm folding/unfolding or eye bulging behaviors he exhibits, I agree, cause him to appear in the throes of a severe Saint Vitus Dance seizure.

This bizarre behavior became manifest *after* he entered coaching and has become increasingly worse over the last twenty years. I recall vividly his demeanor during the initial game he coached as headman. He paced the sidelines, yes, but he only scratched himself. Once. I know because his wife, with whom I was sitting, was mortified he would do this in public. But that was it, one scratch during the entire four quarters! Now, during a game he carries on so that one of the faculty wives actually inquired whether his wife did indeed starch his undershorts. Another felt compelled to suggest the problem might be a laundry detergent to which he is allergic. Poor woman. Coach's wife had to endure a lot for his career!

To be sure, stress aggravates the problem. If you were at the championship game last year, you know what I mean. Our family doctor was in attendance and he became so concerned at the way Coach was behaving, that during the half-time he visited the locker room. He planned to suggest Coach take a sedative. Coach, of course, declined, insisting he "had things under control." This comment did little to allay the physician's concern, for as the good doctor observed Coach's fiery half-time rhetoric while diagramming a "can't miss" play, Coach actually consumed three whole pieces of chalk, just crunched them down like giant *Rolaids*.

I told you he grew up in Vermont, right? Nevertheless, if I had a dollar for every person who has asked me what part of the South Coach comes from, I'd have a lot of money. I can't blame them. Ever listen to him when he says some words: coach is cowch; boy is boaaah; thing is thang; hear is heyaah, and so forth. It's quite a linguistic phenomenon, at least that's what my daughter, who is a linguist calls it. I used to kid Coach about the way his idol, Alabama's legendary Bear Bryant, spoke, but now to hear Coach shout out to a quarterback who failed to get a pass to a receiver, "Boah, you got to braang that thaang, yall heyah, Mistuuh?" you would swear the Bear was shouting it down from his tower. And what's more interesting, this manner of speaking is not confined to the football field. He has never hunted in his life, yet during a bridge game, for example, he'll use expressions like, "I'm as skeered as an ole coon dog" or "hey, dang it paddnah, you're as onery as a treed possum." Why, he has even taken to calling his favorite players names like Bubbah and Hoss. His wife and family finally put their foot down when Coach was considering changing his name from William Matthew Orvis to Billy Mack Orvis. When he asked if the new name didn't sound more "coachish," they all allowed how it sounded more "foolish," and he had just better forget the name change. Everyone on the faculty agreed except Billy Bob Grover, an assistant coach.

Understand, I'm not trying to make excuses for him, but seeking to help people better understand what makes him the way he is. The truth is I believe all these behavioral changes may not have been intentional, that Coach could be the victim of an unrecognized occupational hazard. What is the hazard? Visiting the locker room following a hot August afternoon practice, I could hardly breathe, so heavy and foul was the air. The stench that Coach referred to as "jockmold" was absolutely overpowering. Indeed, the next time I entered the locker room I realized the odor was so palpable and thick, I felt as though I had walked into a bunch of cobwebs, much as one might encounter strolling in a dense forest. My wife and one of our lady friends from church, both a bit straight-laced, couldn't comprehend what I was trying to describe when discussing my odor hypothesis, so during a high school wrestling match, between bouts when no one was paying much attention, I told them to bend down and take a good whiff of the wrestling mat. Sure enough, they came up sputtering, barely able to breathe and while waving their hands before their faces to disperse the noxious fumes both gasped, "Jockmold, all right, jockmold!" My theory is that jockmold is the substance that causes coaches to develop their spastic sideline behaviors.

Fine, but does that explain the speech dialectical changes

you ask? No, but that I believe is readily understood when one considers those who have most influenced Coach's career. You may not be aware of this as most folks aren't, but Coach attended three summer clinics co-hosted by the Bear and Bum Phillips. It was after the third summer that we began to hear boyaah and braang, skeered, the whole ball of wax, so to speak. I'm not placing a value judgement on how these other coaches speak either, just trying to explain Coach's language. A grown man mimicking others, you may think. Why not? Emulation of someone held in high esteem is typical in all professions, so why not coaching? There are those I'm sure who wish he had attended clinics where he would have been influenced by the likes of Bill Walsh and Joe Paterno. But he loved the Bear and Bum and Lord knows, he hasn't exactly been unsuccessful following these role models; 160-40 and eight state division titles isn't exactly shabby. Plus Coach loves his work and his players and they, in turn, love him like a father. He isn't afraid of hard work or sacrifice and is generous to a fault. So I guess what I'm saying is that on balance, no one is really complaining, and I guess we'll all continue to put up with the spastic behaviors and language.

Well, perhaps his wife is entitled to some complaining, a little. Few people realize the sacrifice it takes to be a coach's wife, particularly during the season. Coach felt the following incident was unfair, but I can see his wife's point. Who wouldn't be upset when their Coach-husband arrives home late, like 1:00 A.M. following the Friday night ball game and jumps into bed . . . with his clipboard.

"What's that for," he said she had sleepily inquired.

"To diagram my plays, of course," Coach replied, admitting he was still wired from this evening's close ball game.

Can anyone really blame her for giving him a bit of a blast with her answer, can you not see how it all gets to be a bit much for a wife to bear? I can see why she lost it and responded, "No wonder you never score!"

"Well no, Kevin, you don't exactly have it on the right way, son."

12

THE DAY I VISITED THE GIFTED AND TALENTED CLASSES

My pulse quickened. The building principal, my hostess, hadn't announced it but I felt it — no, knew it. We were approaching the gifted and talented wing! How to explain my prescience? Perhaps it was the way the principal, who moments before seemed harried and overly vigilant, now adopted the self-assured demeanor characteristic of the executives profiled in *MS* magazine. Or was it the bespectacled, briefcase toting lad who rushed by clad in chinos, Docksiders and a Brooks Brothers tweed jacket worn over a tee shirt emblazoned with "HARVARD OR BUST?" Could it have been the abrupt paucity of ripped jean wearers, hand slapping rappers, or the cookie cutter lookalike coeds obviously more concerned with mascara than marks? It doesn't matter how, I knew!

"Cassandra Stemfield-Alcott is our excellent teacher of...."

"Literature," I interrupted the principal, smiling inwardly to myself at her wide-eyed look of surprise.

"But, but, how did you know that?" she asked, her amazement unconcealed.

I nonchalantly shrugged my shoulders while thinking to myself, *Who couldn't have guessed that? Talk about stereotypes. This teacher is an obvious clone of one of her university professors: the artsy, spacey and smugly intellectual type with wild hair, boots, ten stings of necklaces and a huge scarf, a prof who does extensive research on topics like "Hemingway's Use of the Verb 'to be'; Syntactical Symptoms of a Neurotic Personality."*

The professor's progeny spoke: "Melvin, your father's observation that the Little Bo Peep nursery rhyme represents wholesale pirating from the Dead Sea Scrolls is most intriguing and not without merit. Such literary license, I use the term charitably, is not at all unusual I'm sorry to report, class. My own doctoral work seeks to prove that Shakespeare's major plots, the vast body of his work in fact, are taken directly from themes found in Japanese Kabuki, whose dance themes predate the birth of Christ by at least 700 years."

Much student chin stroking and eyeball rolling amid audible "hmms" of approbation elicited a smile of extreme pleasure from the principal who beckoned me to follow. The science labs awaited. I fully expected the white coated, multiple pens in a breast pocket, horn-rim glassed scientist to momentarily declare, "Preparation H contains more of the ingredient..." so precisely did he look the part of the quintessential druggist. No more than a dozen students, similarly attired, were absorbed in a variety of complicated appearing experiments. Suddenly, spying the principal and me, one of the junior editions approached us and loudly proclaimed, "I think I'm on the verge of discovering a cure for Legionnaires Disease, Mrs. B."

"Wonderful news," gushed the principal. "Have you

shared your findings with Professor Gustafson at the university yet?" As she said this, she leaned over to me and as an aside whispered, "He's taking advanced placement pharmacology at the U on Saturdays."

"Yes, but to be candid, I felt his reaction to my request to present the research at the hospital Grand Rounds was most discouraging," he replied.

"Oh, I'm sorry to hear that, Parker."

"I couldn't be scheduled because this year's final guest speakers, Dr. DeBakey and Dr. Jarvik, were previously invited and already announced," continued Parker.

"That doesn't sound exactly fair to me," countered the principal. "After all, you are a home-town product, not to mention one of our most gifted and talented class members. One should think that would count in considering rescheduling an out-of-towner or two. I just hope you aren't being discriminated against because you aren't a full-time medical student."

"My dad's sentiments precisely."

"Well, just don't let any of this get you down, Parker, because we are all terribly proud of the work you are doing. Remember, a prophet is always without honor in his own land," she called to the lad as he returned to his work station.

As the principal and I were moving out the door, she launched into an angry tirade. "Now do you see why I'm so defensive about our G and T program? To put it in Rodney Dangerfield's words, we don't get any respect. I'm about ready to go public with the attitude of people around here. I'll bet *Sixty Minutes* would love to do a piece on this."

We reached the fine arts wing and entered the orchestral rehearsal room. The conductor, a dead ringer for Leopold Stokowski, wild white mane and all, was in the process of reproving two crest-fallen violin virtuosi standing before the rest of the orchestra.

"I ope you not let rave notices in *New York Times* las'

Sunday to your head going, making bigheadness," said the conductor in broken English.

"No maestro, it's just that while doing a walk-the-baby with my yoyo, the string cut my finger and, as you are aware the Paganini requires inordinate string pressure, particularly at the Adagio," replied the spokesman for the two players.

"Yah, now dees hees good. Yoyo Ma heem you should try to follow. Okay. Now again, from the Coda, page two."

"What is the..." I started to ask, but the principal put a finger to her nose to silence me and at the same time inclined her head toward the door. Once out in the corridor she explained, "I hope you don't think me rude but the Maestro does not brook so much as a cough during a rehearsal. A whisper is cause for a tirade. He recently threw a baton at the School Board chairman for having the temerity to speak during a rehearsal."

"What happened to the maestro for doing that?"

"The maestro?" she asked incredulously. "You mean what happened to the chairman? He tried to appease the maestro by immediately submitting his resignation from the Board. The maestro, however, graciously accepted his apology and the whole thing, fortunately, blew over. But it was touch and go there for a while."

"Oh, I wouldn't have believed the maestro would have that kind of clout," I then said.

"Maestros for the gifted and talented don't grow on trees or in teacher training institutions either. We can always get a new chairman, but not a maestro," countered the principal.

"What does the regular orchestra teacher do?" I then asked.

"Teaches non G and T kids."

"Where do they practice?" I asked.

"Either in the boiler room or out in the bus garage, depending on whether the boilers are down or if there are buses to overhaul," responded my guide. "Ah, here we are. *Excuse, Madame.*"

We had reached the language room and the last part of the principal's comment was addressed to the French teacher.

"*Mais oui,*" replied Madame in a Parisian accented soft voice. "Ees the gentleman who geeves money for the class trip to Paree, no?"

After explaining that I was a visitor to the class and not a prospective donor, the three of us chatted briefly and then the principal and I were off to return to her office. "Sorry about Madame asking if you were a donor. You see, all of the G and T students in French are going to spend the summer in total immersion speaking only French, in Paris of course. That is if we can raise the final $10,000 of the $40,000 goal we set. We are confident we will, by the way."

"Those kids are not only gifted and talented but lucky, too," I answered, just a bit testily. "I just wish my time today wasn't so limited, I would have loved to have spoken with some of the children," I continued in a warmer tone of voice.

"Yes," replied the principal. "The first-graders you saw today are exceptional, but I think you will also be impressed visiting grades 2 through 6."

13

THE LADY WITH THE LICKABLE FACE

W ell, today I did it. I licked the face of the Home Ec teacher. Understandably, she was not sure at first whether or not this was a compliment, but when I explained my reasons for doing it she was actually flattered.

"You always look so tidy, clean and shiny that today I couldn't help myself," was the way I explained it. But it is more than this. I did it for professional reasons. Let me put it this way. If a contest were held to pick the perfect model for a Home Ec teacher recruitment poster, Deanna would win hands down.

Deanna is the epitome of good grooming, perfectly made up, and she always carries herself with poise. I so admire her professional demeanor and excellent teaching reputation. Plus, she also adds color to the faculty. It seems like every other day, certainly every other week, she dons a corsage-like decorative ornamentation highlighting the particular season or holiday soon to be celebrated.

Let's see, I remember fall fun: dried acorns, leaves, and mums. Halloween hoopla: a mini jack-o-lantern, black broom riding witch and slanty-eyed cat. Thanksgiving thoughts: a colorful turkey, Pilgrim hat and cornucopia. Christmas, of course, you get the picture. I have heard Deanna referred to as a walking calendar, not a bad description if I must say so myself.

Unquestionably Deanna has brought the Home Ec classes from lightly regarded, poorly attended, solidly female offerings in sewing and homemaking to highly regarded, oversubscribed courses with intriguing titles like "Bachelor/Bachelorette Living", "Cooking for One" and "Woks, Processors, and The Use of Other Magical Culinary Tools." Clearly Julia Child has nothing on our Deanna; neither does the Pied Piper judging by the number of boys now outnumbering the girls in these classes.

It is such a joy to visit the Home Ec room. You walk in and there, happily stirring, sauteing and whisking are some of the school's most infamous characters. Last week, for example, I visited and immediately one of them rushed over to me and while still stirring up a storm says, "Hey, Dr. Clements, want to smell something outrageous, man?"

"Sure Gonzo," I replied, deeply inhaling odors of a surprising inoffensive smelling concoction rising from the bowl now deposited within a micrometer of my nostrils. "Hmmm, dynamite," I further lied. "What is it?"

"Pepperoni angel cake," he replied. "Too bad you can't have a taste, right?" With that he yanks away the **prize** recipe.

Thank goodness, I think to myself, while outwardly feigning profound disappointment over his denial to let me sample the delicacy.

This brings me to the licking. It is obvious Deanna's work

called for some appreciation despite the notoriously bad concoctions that came out of the Home Ec kitchens. It used to be my habit to go in and sample, usually brownies, twice a month. I thought no harm would come from this even though my mentor, a wise old now retired superintendent, warned me otherwise. His simple advice: Don't eat there! He further opined that should decorum or a student's self image be at stake, accept what was proffered, stating you are going to save it for later, then on your way down the hall give the food to the first student you encounter. They are always hungry, particularly the boys.

Perhaps you question my behavior? Not after frequent bouts of constipation and considering the fact youths' intestinal functions are far more resilient than those approaching social security age. Face it, we're talking survival here. I know whereof I speak. Six months ago I accepted a cupcake in Home Ec and, without thinking, gobbled it down. I am still bound up! I am getting desperate, too. These days I do not drink orange juice in the morning, but have taken to doing four ounces of *Mazola Oil*. I have done prunes, *Milk of Magnesia*, wheat bran, you name it, but nothing has helped. Do not laugh, either. My eyes used to be blue, not their present burnt sienna.

Alas, the lady with the lickable face has not been able to substitute "finger licking good" for "lick your finger, it's as good," but no matter. The faculty would be considerably less effective without Deanna, and certainly less colorful. Indeed, I for one would far less enjoy going to school everyday. So you see, rather than eat to demonstrate my professional admiration, I licked her face.

"Bet he would never lick a shop teacher's face," charges a social studies teacher who I am convinced will not be happy until I am either flogged publicly or fired — or both. She is right about the shop teachers! How could you consider licking someone covered with sawdust and wood chips, someone in a uniform like elevator repair persons wear? No, lickableness and shop teachers are definitely incompatible.

And so it goes, the public controversy continues. It is crazy since Deanna, as I stated earlier, has forgiven me, but still the hullabaloo persists. Frankly, I am convinced outside agitation is what it is about. It appears, however, the superintendent does not want the whole thing to get blown up any further, so I guess I am going to have to swallow my pride, and even though I do not feel I have anything to apologize for, I will make a public apology to Deanna before the entire faculty, K-12. But my flexibility has limits: under no circumstances will I agree to stop making humorous remarks about the food Deanna's kids produce or agree to eat it. After all, to paraphrase the old sticks and stones jingle, *cupcakes and cookies will bind my bowels, but licking never hurt anything.*

© Zach Clements, 1990

"*I wouldn't go trying to win any haute cuisine contests, but as cafeteria food goes, we can trot along side the Galloping Gourmet, if you catch my drift, hon.*"

14

A NEW SOURCE OF GUIDANCE COUNSELOR WISDOM

Professional educators are presently living in an era of parental discontent. Though superintendents vociferously proclaim they suffer the preponderance of parental abuse, I would argue guidance counselors are the hands-down winners of this dubious honor.

It's the no-win nature of the counselor's role that does 'em in! Every day students present them with a cornucopia of problems ranging from dropping algebra or acid to insights on the merits of studying zoology or Zionism; counselors literally deal with concerns from A to Z! The difficulty of the role is compounded by the fact that each client's dilemma is intensely personal, a crisis demanding an answer — NOW! But . . . the solution given Mary doesn't work for Murray. Taking time to think is viewed as indecisiveness, while a from-the-hip judgment elicits charges of rashness. Every comment, much less an answer, is found lacking, ultimately adding to growing parental discontent.

Could it be — perish the thought — guidance counselors are following the wrong gurus? Perhaps Freud, Adler, Dreikurs, Rogers and Glasser are not the wellsprings of wisdom counselor trainers in graduate school reputed them to be. At the risk of being labeled a heretic, I humbly commend to my colleagues' attention a new champion, a bona fide oracle: Benjamin Franklin. His *Poor Richard's Almanac*, a sparkling little gem, is described in the book's foreword as containing the "choicest morsels of wisdom," a description with which I enthusiastically concur. Admittedly a dyed-in-the-wool Franklinphile, it is no overstatement when I declare this well known savant offers counselors many perfect rejoinders that will cause parents and students to regard guidance personnel with new-found respect. Consider the following examples:

Parent: What do you think I ought to tell my daughter when she asks — no, tells me — she is thinking of having sexual relations with her steady boyfriend?

Counselor: "If Passion drives, let Reason hold the reins."

Parent: My "preppy" daughter wants to know why she shouldn't be seen with the "burnouts" at school if she chooses. What should I tell her?

Counselor: "Glass, China, and Reputation are easily cracked and never well-mended," or "She that lieth down with dogs shall rise up with fleas."

Parent: My child refuses to heed my advice, about not trying to step into other people's arguments. Any ideas for help?

Counselor: "Those who in quarrels interpose, must often wipe a bloody nose."

Parent: My daughter thinks that having a smart answer and being quick on the uptake are going to make earning a living a snap. Give me a rejoinder, please.

Counselor: "There are many witty persons whose brains can't fill their bellies."

Parent: Our kids think that because their grandparents might leave them a large estate, they've got it made. How can I help them realize this is bad thinking?

Counselor: "Many a person would have been worse if his Estate had been better."

Parent: Our son has the mistaken idea that he can borrow money again and again because those from whom he borrowed have probably forgotten. I've got to wise him up.

Counselor: "Creditors have better memories than debtors."

Parent: My teenagers act like using jokes can get them through any situation. Help me save him much grief.

Counselor: "Thou cannot joke an enemy into a friend, but thou may a friend into an enemy."

Parent: Our kids only seem to learn a lesson after they screw up royally. What can we say to save them grief?

Counselor: "Wise people learn by others' mistakes; fools learn by their own."

Parent: My son says he's going to get involved in a "rumble" at school. What do you suggest I tell him?

Counselor: "Paintings and Fightings are best seen at a distance," or better, "Wars bring Scars."

Parent: My son keeps getting low marks because he is always shouting out the wrong answers in class. Any suggestions?

Counselor: "Tis better to be thought a fool than to open your mouth and erase all shadow of a doubt."

Parent: My child doesn't appreciate all the important practical things concerning drugs and decision-making that you are trying to get across to him. Why do you think this is so?

Counselor: "Good Sense is a thing all need, few have, and none think they want."

Parent: My son thinks he's going to just hang around and do nothing after he graduates. Any suggestions?

Counselor: "Laziness travels so slowly that Poverty soon overtakes him."

The foregoing were but a few of Ben's wise observations that are as relevant today as they were 200 years ago. I commend them to guidance counselors' attention and suggest they read *Poor Richard's Almanac* to acquire additional enlightenment. If after such reading, followed by application of your new-found wisdom, parents or students continue to be unhappy with counselors' suggestions, let one of Franklin's witticisms buoy their spirits: "Most people return small favours, acknowledge middling ones, and repay great ones with ingratitude."

"Now, if you could just give me a clue as to what your outside of school interests are, it would greatly assist me in helping you plan your future."

15

THE ANNUAL RUNNING OF
THE SCHOOLHOUSE STAKES

F all is in the air and to learning fans that can mean only one thing, the oldest classic in the sport of building educated citizens, the Schoolhouse Stakes. This event, a grueling ten-month test, annually benefits well over 50,000,000 children who hail from every socio-economic level and every town, city and hamlet throughout the land. At stake, the Job Entree Trophy and the even more coveted College Entry Cup which carries with it an invitation to compete in the Higher Education Derby, a four-year test of skill, intelligence and, in the eyes of many people, luck.

Each year billions of dollars are invested in the Schoolhouse at the local levels while the heavy hitters in Washington add additional billions at the federal level. Historians who have covered the event for many years feel these figures would be significantly higher were it not for a number of retired and disgruntled fans, who not only refuse to back any of the expected entries, but have also done their best to tarnish the entire event. Over its 225 plus year history, the Schoolhouse Stakes has shown a steady increase in purses and is now, at long last, one of the Nation's richest contests, along with The Defense Spending Derby, The Foreign Aid Futurity, The Consumer Spending Cup, The Alcohol Annual and the Tobacco Trot.

Unfortunately, some of the pageantry normally associated with the Schoolhouse is annually dampened by societal conditions. Among the most recent culprits are the Stock Market Crash and the Budget Deficit. These join other well-remembered classic party poopers: Energy Crisis, Rate of Inflation and Economic Recession. Veteran Stakes watchers are quick to point out, however, through good times and bad, peace and war, this event has *never* been cancelled.

How does this year's field shape up for a big race? As usual, the entries will include a mixed bag that could produce a few surprises. First, a brief survey of the top entries:

Back to Basics

An entry from the Save A Dollar Stables, BASICS was sired by TAXPAYERS DILEMMA out of SOARING TAXES and is the grandson of DISGRUNTLED SOCIETY and PUBLIC'S LAST STAND. After strong performances several years back, this nostalgia-evoking gamer has once more regained his excellent form and figures to attract extensive conservative backing and has to be considered a solid contender.

Programs For the Gifted

The pride of the Save The Smarty Stables, this relative newcomer to the Stakes has long been the champion thoroughbred in the Private School Dash and the Parochial Invitational. A descendant of STANDARDS PRESERVATION and that great champion ACADEMIC EXCELLENCE, this entry is expected to attract increased backing from trendy venues and the pushy variety of bettors. Insiders hasten to point out that the horse has already been overworked and could likely collapse under the rigorous pace of the Stakes.

Mainstreaming

This gelding out of UNCLOSETING THE HANDICAPPED was sired by SOCIETAL CONSCIOUSNESS. After a big win in the U.S. Congress several years back this horse followed up with a number of impressive victories, thanks to the backing of the Feds and most state legislatures. Those in the know fear this support is now mostly of the verbal variety and lacks hard cash on the nose.

Competency Based Standards

A stallion sired by VOTE CONSCIOUS LEGISLATORS out of UNWORKABLE SOLUTIONS carries the colors of the Quiet The Public Farms. Handicappers feel this one has the look of a champion but lacks heart and despite the whip, will likely falter when up against the three spoilers mentioned later in this report.

The following entries are considered dark horses that have the potential to go all the way but will more likely be stalking horses or rabbits for the rest of the field.

Teacher's Union

Frequently disruptive at the start, often delaying the event and angering the fans, this entry has been coming on in recent years, usually turning in solid performances once out of the blocks. While many backers belittle this one's bloodlines, ECONOMIC STANDARDS and NEGOTIATION POWER with distant relations in QUALITY EDUCATION and CONCERN FOR STUDENTS, this horse has firm backing by track insiders throughout the land.

Restricted Budgets

The stout hearted filly, a daughter of TAXPAYER REVOLT and FRILLESS LEARNING and also a direct descendant of CUTS TO EDUCATION, is expected to challenge from the start and will test the endurance, will power and patience of all. However, RECOGNITION OF REALITY and ESCALATING COSTS, two other veteran geldings of many previous Stakes races, are expected to again box this lady against the rail.

The following are two late entries that are surprises in that many felt they just lacked enough experience to compete against this mature field.

Effective Schools

A strong finisher that seems to have caught the fancy of stable managers across the country, this horse sired by SCHOOLS OF EXCELLENCE out of COMMON SENSE is proving quite popular in the early wagering this year. If popularity and being "in" (particularly with the Washington set) is any criteria, then this horse bears watching.

White House Recognition

At one time considered bound for Stakes immortality, this entry has been the object of much questioning. Age, bloodlines and veracity of performance stats have been the major sources of contention. Out of BLAME THE SCHOOLS, the daughter of POLITICAL RHETORIC, this sprinter can't go the distance, despite colorful ceremonies of the past.

The following three entries are given practically no chance of winning but are universally believed to be potential spoilers.

Tenor Of the Times
Social Issues
Student Apathy

These three entries, all bearing the colors of the Societal Realities Stables, are powerful pace horses that critics say should be barred from the race because of repeated charges of "tampering" and "unsportsmanlike conduct" during previous outings. Nonetheless, these three will be in the field and, while not regarded as contenders of the serious variety, must be considered a threat to any of the other horses in the field, particularly those not used to bumping, boxing, or other "hard-nosed tactics." These three are definitely outside possibilities if the track is sloppy, as has been the case over recent Stakes events.

In closing this survey of the field, special mention must be made of the greatest long shot of this year as in past years, everyone's sentimental favorite, QUALITY PUBLIC SCHOOLS. A gallant trooper over the years, this entry is from the Founding Fathers Stables which gave us those all-time champions, DECLARATION OF INDEPENDENCE, BILL OF RIGHTS and LAND OF HOPE, plus legendary giants among trainers, George Washington, Thomas Jefferson and Abraham Lincoln. This strong-willed filly is the daughter of BACKBONE OF DEMOCRACY and the fabled HOPE OF THE FUTURE. It is common knowledge that she has never reached her full potential and is expected this year to attract even less backing than in past years. Be that as it may, this writer and others who wager with their hearts and conscience still consider this sentimental non-quitter a horse to be reckoned with. Indeed, with some additional backing and encouragement, along with the right track conditions, this lady could just fool everybody and meet the needs of students and society by winning the whole thing.

But don't bet on it!

EPILOGUE

I am happy to report that despite seemingly endless reports of their imminent demise, public schools are alive and well. The overwhelming majority of schools I visit are positive places for people to work and for children to learn. Unhappily, there are some schools where negativism and pessimism dwell, but I can assure you these are the exception, not the rule.

Positive schools do not just happen, they are not accidental flukes. An attractive physical plant, adequate supplies and a satisfactory salary schedule certainly help, but these alone do not guarantee an upbeat atmosphere. Indeed, "the big three" are sometimes present but the spark is still missing! Also, contrary to what many critics allege, positive schools do not only set high academic achievement as their foremost goal; participation in sports, clubs and other non-academic interests are also given high priority. If excellent test scores, higher than average teacher salaries, a proliferation of snazzy materials or a new building are not sufficient clues, what then causes the refrain "there is no place on earth I would rather be" to run through my head as I enter a school?

A contagious spirit permeates the air, catching to students and visitors alike. It flows from the staff who appear to be happy with their work. Energies are expended on making the most of the existing facility and available materials instead of continually bemoaning what cannot be changed. Concerns are expressed in a businesslike manner. Individual and group contributions are acknowledged and appreciated. Belonging and involvement on the part of both students and staff are readily apparent. In short, the staff communicates this is a good place to work, which in turn is echoed by the actions of the students. What a great place to be!

When I see smiles and hear laughter I know this is a school where it is commonplace to hear people say, "I'm proud to be a teacher." I love to tour such buildings; I look forward to meeting you.